Editorial

T0303494

Heraclitus is wrong. As we get older we walk into the same river twice, a third and fourth time, and we have the same illumination we had before. It's the first time all over again.

Back in *PN Review* 42, Jorge Luis Borges wrote,

> A.C. Bradley said that one of the effects of poetry is that it gives us the impression not of discovering something new but of remembering something we have forgotten. When we read a good poem we imagine that we too could have written it; that the poem already existed within us. This brings us to the Platonic definition of poetry: that winged, fickle, sacred thing. As a definition it is fallible, since that winged, fickle, sacred thing could also be music (except that poetry is a form of music). Plato, defining poetry, gives us an example of poetry. And this brings us to the idea that poetry is an aesthetic experience: something that would be a revolution in the teaching of poetry.

This revolution keeps almost beginning, then being deferred or deflected by theories, contexts, or subordinated to biography. The enactments a great poem achieves are obscured by descriptive discourse and interpretation. Borges has a wonderful poem (quoted before more than once in these pages) about the first sonnet and sonneteer, 'Un Poeta del Siglo XIII' ('A Poet of the Thirteenth Century'). This poet shuffles through the drafts of his poem. It is about to become the very first, not yet recognised, sonnet. He plays against the emerging form. Perhaps he has sensed, says the poem, radiating *from the future*, 'a rumour of far-off nightingales', things to come, even of impending clichés. The sonnet asks in the sestet:

> Had he realised that he was not alone,
> that a cryptic, an inscrutable Apollo
> had revealed to him an archetypal pattern,
>
> a greedy crystal that would detain,
> as night detains day and then lets it go:
> Dedalus, labyrinth, the riddle, Laius son.

The future weighs on the present, much as the past can do: looking back, we see the past is aware of and returns our gaze. Prolepsis, analepsis, arrest the quill of the soon-to-be-sonneteer. A momentous little moment, a defining one. That first sonnet is recognised by its poet, not a discovery but a gift from 'the inscrutable Apollo'. Classical myth, legend, literature, common memory provide content. The poet, suspended between a classical *then* and a modern *now*, mediates. The modern reader does the same. 'Each later sonnet in whatever language participates in his work, and he in its. A poet who develops received forms is always in collaboration with the poems that came before and those that will come after. A sonnet never belongs exclusively to its author. Or even to its language. It is a given, a gift, in Italian, French (all the Frenches alive today), German, Englishes.'

Christopher Middleton turns to Bradley, too. 'The poet speaks to us of one thing, but in this one thing there seems to lurk the secret of all... which, we feel, would satisfy not only the imagination, but the whole of us.' It's a brilliant observation, but categorical. The sense we experience of 'the secret of all' visits us infrequently, cannot be faked, and when it comes it is powerful, implausible, illuminating. In his essay 'Notes on a Viking Prow' (*PN Review* 10), to which I return so often, Middleton addressed the theme head on. He writes:

> To recapture poetic reality in a tottering world, we may have to revise, once more, the idea of a poem as an expression of the 'contents' of a subjectivity. Some poems, at least, and some types of poetic language, constitute structures of a singularly radiant kind, where 'self-expression' has undergone a profound change of function. We experience these structures, if not as revelations of being, then as apertures upon being. We experience them as we experience nothing else.

Middleton's argument is hortatory, not polemical, pulling back the corner on a creative possibility which looks new but is in fact the *fons et origo* of all creative work with language. He had Whitman in mind, among others, and his essay which starts in archaeology ends in the vivid presences that language discloses.

Coleridge, like Middleton a great English Germanist, preserved some galumphing hexameters dedicated to 'Dear William and dear Dorothea'. Why would he keep such words? The otherwise unfortunate fragment concludes with a kind of Whitmanesque openness, or openingness.

> ... my eyes are a burthen,
> Now unwillingly closed, now open and aching with darkness.
> O! what a life is the eye! what a strange and inscrutable essence!
> Him that is utterly blind, nor glimpses the fire that warms him;
> Him that never beheld the swelling breast of his mother;
> Him that smiled in his gladness as a babe that smiles in its slumber;
> Even for him it exists, it moves and stirs in its prison;
> Lives with a separate life, and 'Is it a Spirit?' he murmurs:
> 'Sure it has thoughts of its own, and to see is only a language.'

Not a great or even a good passage of poetry, but one does not ask that kind of excellence from such sustained clarity of language, of seeing. It is different in kind from other verse, with a linguistic consistency and authority all its own, at once because *and* regardless of its subject matter, echoes and allusions. It is not so far from this to 'Kubla Khan' and 'The Rhyme of the Ancient Mariner'. They come from another realm, are in a different register from poems of his which respond to prose analysis, can be taken apart and reassembled, that have design and designs on their addressees and respond to paraphrase. 'Kubla Khan' *occurs*. It is not an act of the poet's conscious will but of a shared imagination. Coleridge never knew where it came from and could never secure another poem from that source. '"Is it a Spirit?" he murmurs.'

Words have first and second intentions, Walter Pater said, and a poem built on second intentions can contain that Spirit. Think of Emily Dickinson's 'The Heart Asks Pleasure First', or take this speech from *Measure for Measure* where the second intentions are embodied in echo and etymology, as in the emboldened words.

> Ay, but to die, and go we know not where;
> To lie in cold obstruction, and to rot;
> This sensible warm motion to become
> A kneaded clod; and the de-lighted spirit
> To bathe in fiery floods, or to reside
> In thrilling region of thick-ribbèd ice;
> To be imprisoned in the viewless winds
> And blown with restless violence round about
> The pendant world; or to be worse than worst
> Of those that lawless and incertain thought
> Imagine howling –

Letters to the editor

The French Connection
On Translating Miodrag Pavlović

James Sutherland-Smith writes: Chris Miller's 'Constructing Pavlović' (*PN Review* 272) is an attempt to draw attention to the poetry of Miodrag Pavlović, one of the three great modernists of Serbian poetry, the other two being Vasko Popa and Ivan Lalić. However, despite my own pique at his dismissive comment on my and Nenad Aleksić's translations, for me the article is based on what is a rather narrow selection from Pavlović's range of poetry.

The first translation into English was the New Rivers Press chapbook of 1976 by the remarkable multilingual translator Joachim Neugroschel (1938–2011). It was called *The Conqueror in Constantinople* and featured translations of twenty-two poems from the collections *Milk of Origins* and *Great Scythia*. Versions of all of these appear in the larger selection by Barry Callaghan, *A Voice Locked in Stone* (Exile Editions, 1985). Bernard Johnson's *The Slavs Beneath Parnassus* (Angel and New Rivers, 1985) has translations of twelve of Neugroschel's selection. In addition, Callaghan and Johnson have versions of two further poems in common.

Now, either the three translators are to be congratulated on homing in on twelve or so essential poems, or there is a French connection lurking in the background. If so, this might well be a wholly benign individual, a French poet, Robert Marteau (1925–2011), who was a close friend of Pavlović and his translator into French. Neugroschel in his translator's note indicates that he had no Serbian and translated from Marteau's versions; '(they) were so startling that I proceeded to turn them into English'. The Callaghan versions have an afterword by Robert Marteau translated into English, and Callaghan doesn't indicate how he arrived at his versions. Perhaps Miller would not have attempted his hybrid translations of extracts using Johnson and Marteau's translations had he been aware of the reduplication of Neugroschel's original translations.

Miller is wildly off target in his extract from 'Svetovid Speaks'. It should be 'Baltic' not 'Balkans' and the idiom 'kovati zaveru' means 'hatch a plot'. Neugroschel (and I assume Marteau in French) is spot on here. To twist the knife further, Callaghan's version of 'Putnik na odlasku' (Traveller's Departure) is at least faithful to Pavlović's versification. Miller's 'The Traveller Departs' is not.

Both Callaghan and Johnson produced further translations. In 1983 Callaghan had published *Singing at the Whirlpool* (Exile Editions) and in 1989 Johnson published *Links*, also with Exile editions, incidentally the imprint Callaghan founded. Both are translations from a much sparer style of poetry where Pavlović explores prehistory revealed by the results of archaeology on Neolithic sites in Serbia, long before either Greeks, Romans or Slavic people arrived. This change in style for a significant part of Pavlović's poetry is not mentioned by Miller and neither is his late religious poetry in prose forms.

Concentrating on a style of poetry, as Miller does, written in the late 1960s and early 1970s and fashionable in the Penguin Modern Poetry series does Miodrag Pavlović's reputation little service.

Chris Miller replies: James has the privilege and authority of an acquaintance with Serbian. I know of the Neugroschel chapbook, but have never seen it; it is not in any Oxford library and was commercially unaffordable. Marteau's versions have indeed proved inspiring! 'Balkan' for 'Baltic' *is* a grave error, for which I apologise; 'weave a conspiracy' for 'hatch a plot' less so. I have some examples of Pavlović's shorter, sparer poems, but have not been persuaded by them even in Marteau's translations. My object was to interest readers and, ideally, translators, in Pavlović and in the poems by him that I love. I eagerly await convincing translations of Pavlović's other styles.

Serendipity

Beverley Bie Brahic writes: *PNR* 274 landed on my Paris doormat this week and leafing through it (am I the only person who reads magazines back to front?) I discovered Sinéad Morrissey's tribute to Ciaran Carson. I keep copies of Morrissey's *On Balance* on two continents; I carry a copy of Carson's *Still Life* around with me so I was ready to be impressed by Morrissey's thoughtful, as well as witty, enviably precise and deliciously personal comments about Carson's 'non-linearity' and 'rambling ambiguity' in *The Star Factory*, a book I don't know, but have just ordered through Paris's Red Wheelbarrow bookstore.

May I add that reading Morrissey's poems, it has more than once crossed my mind that she would be an excellent candidate for the Oxford Poetry Professorship. Her Carson lecture confirms that intuition. I am hoping that somewhere down the line she will be nominated and have the courage to accept.

Meanwhile I am very much looking forward to A.E. Stallings's turn in the chair.

News & Notes

John Weir • *Roger Hickin writes:* It was a lucky day for the New Zealand poet James K. Baxter when a young poet who was training for the priesthood wrote to him in 1959. The two soon struck up a close friendship and when Baxter died at the age of forty-six in 1972, it was Father John Weir who became the tireless and meticulous editor of major collections of Baxter's writings, a task which would occupy him for the next fifty years.

Under Weir's editorship three volumes of previously uncollected and unpublished Baxter poems appeared in the 1970s, followed by the first *Collected Poems* in 1979, the multiple-volume editions of *Complete Prose* in 2015, *Letters of a Poet* in 2019, *Complete Poems* in 2022 and *The Selected Poems* in 2023 – the last a definitive selection made from the more than three thousand poems that comprise Baxter's literary legacy.

Weir's own poetry was published in four collections between 1963 and 1983: *The Sudden Sun*, *The Iron Bush*, *A Warning against Water-Drinkers* and *Treading Water*, as well as a final collection, *Sparks among the Stubble* (2021). Unlike Baxter, who was always a monologist, Weir was an engaging and generous conversationalist. He was a kind man with a formidable intellect, whose as yet unpublished monographs on Gerald Manley Hopkins and Lewis Carroll combine exceptional scholarship and acute poetic insight.

John Weir was born in Nelson on 25 April 1935 and died in Christchurch on 27 December 2023.

This was one of his last poems:

It's alright if

It's alright if
the morning rose doesn't shimmer
at the window
to be viewed intently
or if the same wind that stirs just now
among the dark pines that fight
their customary rearguard action
later humphs and fusses over
strutting roosters in backyards
and private vestments and socks hanging
on lines that stretch from
the Golden Age of Queen Victoria till now
or if the white waterfall
pouring silently over the edge of the world
disposes of some who lingered once
at the tipping-point of now
only to become grafted to the veins
that blush from somewhere to
our always on the point of faltering hearts.

It's alright if
such things happen because
how could it be otherwise?

David Ferry • *Greg Miller writes:* David Ferry died on 5 November, in Lexington, Massachusetts, at the age of ninety-nine. Ferry's most prolific period as a poet came after he retired from Wellesley College at the age of sixty-five; he published two books of poetry before, and five after. Ferry won the National Book Award in 1986 at the age of eighty-six for *Bewilderment: New Poems and Translations*. *Of No Country I Know: New and Selected Poems and Translations* (1999) won the Lenore Marshall Prize, the Bingham Poetry Prize and the Bobbitt National Prize for Poetry from the Library of Congress. Alan Shapiro, in his preface to this book of new and selected poems, writes that Ferry 'is one of those rare poets who seems, as we see his poetry working out its concerns, to grow younger and wiser at the same time. He is a great poet and this is a great book.' *Some Things I Said*, Ferry's final book of poems, will be published in December. Many consider Ferry's translation of the epic *Gilgamesh* the best of our time; he also translated Horace's *Odes* and Virgil's *Eclogues*, *Georgics* and the *Aeneid.* Born in Orange, New Jersey on 5 March 1924, Ferry was married to the critic Anne Ferry until her death in 2006; she wrote seven books of criticism, including *The Title to the Poem*, awarded the Christian Gauss Prize. (Ferry credited his wife for the titles of most of his books.) Ferry's most memorable lyrics focus unflinchingly and without sentimentality on the dispossessed. The poems bespeak the man's profound humanity.

The last poem in *Dwelling Place* went uncollected: 'Envoi':

Let these not be the black, imaginary
flowers of hell, nihilotropic,
turning their iron faces toward
no light but the light of the dead letter.

Refaat Alareer • In the *Bookseller* of 12 December 2023, Ra Page of Comma Press paid tribute to the Palestinian poet Refaat Alareer, killed in an air strike on Gaza City the week before. 'Alareer was a professor of comparative literature at the Islamic University of Gaza and a founding collaborator for We Are Not Numbers (WANN), a storytelling project through which international writers mentor young Palestinians to "tell the stories behind the numbers of Palestinians in the news". He edited *Gaza Writes Back: Short Stories from Young Writers in Gaza, Palestine* (Just World Books) and had been working with Comma Press on a superhero project, as well as a project with the *Washington Post* to build a collective literary "memory map" to commemorate lost places in the Strip.' Page described the poet as 'Above all else, [...] generous. He always championed others, ahead of himself. He was a great writer, but his mission was to support and give a platform to others. We had the honour of spending a lot of time with him in Gaza last year, driving around in his funny little car – definitely the smallest, most peculiar car in Gaza – listening to audiobooks and podcasts on his sound system, and trying to translate hilarious Palestinian idioms into English rhyming couplets. He was gracious, gentle, patient and funny. He had a wicked sense of humour and no fear of the perpetrators of lies and double-speech, two attributes that might have got him killed. [...] Refaat's legacy will be the way he has exposed the lunacy of this age. People are more concerned about "performing" an empty morality than actually being moral.'

Pam Bailey, co-founder of WANN, said: 'When I set out to find the best writing coach in Gaza to join We Are Not Numbers, Refaat was universally called out by both students and graduates. He was tough, but kind; strict, but flexible. Above all, he was fiercely passionate about preserving Palestinian culture and sharing it with the world through the power of the word and, as he said in his last poem, the teacher's "marker".'

Benjamin Zephaniah • Benjamin Obadiah Iqbal Zephaniah, who died at sixty-five, identified himself as a 'writer, lyricist, musician and naughty boy'. As a boy, one of eight siblings born of a Jamaican nurse and Bajan postman, he suffered from paternal violence and a deeply unsettled upbringing. He was humorous, insubordinate, angry. There was time spent in detention and jail. Zephaniah wrote and performed his way out and up, working with his communities and making his way to the big smoke where he began to find success and wider connection.

His rhyming can remind us of the Irish-born Scottish master of public performance, an entertainer in his own day with bold public themes and convictions, William Topaz McGonagall, in its performative abandon and some of its effects, but in Zephaniah's case this was self-conscious and deliberate. He was born in Birmingham, and his written, spoken and performed language had the inflections of his birthplace enhanced with other accents and tones, primarily Caribbean to which he was entitled. He knew Hindi, Mandarin and Urdu and spoke up for other now British languages.

Zephaniah became a darling of parts of the establishment, in part because of his outspokenness, his dreadlocks and his engaging contrariness. A BBC poll discovered that he was the third favourite poet 'of all time' in Britain, and he became an honorary fellow of the British Academy and was mooted as a possible poet laureate. He might have been the Oxford Professor of Poetry if it hadn't been for Seamus Heaney. Zephaniah collected over fifteen honorary doctorates, even more than Dame Edith Sitwell. But he famously refused an OBE in 2003. 'I am profoundly anti-Empire', he declared to Mr Blair and Mrs Queen. In *PN Review* we published a harsh letter from James Sutherland-Smith: 'I was surprised by your approval of Benjamin Zephaniah's refusal of the OBE (*PNR* 155). Perhaps I've become irremediably cynical, but it seemed to me that the gesture was of benefit to Benjamin Zephaniah only, the restatement of an easily won cliché by somebody who is a cliché himself. No doubt his agent is well pleased, if I may use an ancient intensifier. Zephaniah has undertaken workshops and visits outside Britain as a British Council writer-in-residence. The British Council, it is pertinent to restate, received a royal charter and coat of arms from King George VI and receives money from Parliament, which constitutionally is approved by the reigning monarch. So, Zephaniah may have refused a medal from Her Majesty the Queen, but he has definitely accepted her shilling.'

The Black Writers' Guild, which he helped to found, praised this 'titan of British literature'. For many writers from a variety of communities he was an enabling example, a changer of a status quo. In 1980, Page One Books, a co-operative, published his *Pen Rhythm*. Zephaniah established a national platform by means of Channel 4. Publications (novels, plays and other writings) and performances around the country and indeed the world followed. Nelson Mandela invited Zephaniah to lead a concert at the Royal Albert Hall when he paid his first state visit to Britain in 1996.

He loved the freedom he gained from books. 'You can go anywhere you like, and if there's a destination you want to go to and you can't see it, create it. Write it. Tell your story.' Judith Palmer, director of the Poetry Society, noted how 'His poems packed a punch for social justice'. His death was the occasion for dozens of obituaries, tributes and a celebration of the difference his example had made to British culture.

Seven years for poems • On 29 December Al Jazeera reported on the detention and sentencing of two Russian poets charged with 'undermining national security' by reciting poems against the Russian war on the Ukraine. Artyom Kamardin, thirty-three, and Yegor Shtovba, twenty-three, will spend long spells in prison. Their recitation took place during an anti-mobilisation protest. The Kremlin has not let up on its prosecution of dissent. Kamardin will serve seven years in jail. He read at a demonstration after Putin mobilised 300,000 reservists when Russia was back-footed in 2022. The move was greeted by widespread opposition which was quickly stifled. Kamardin's offending poem was entitled 'Kill me, militia man!' and ended, Al Jazeera said, '"Glory to Kievan Rus, Novorossiya – suck!" – using the historic terms for Ukraine's capital Kyiv and a term from days of the Russian Empire that Moscow uses for the area of southeastern Ukraine it is trying to annex, respectively'. Days after the event, Amnesty International reports, 'police beat and violated Kamardin with a dumbbell before forcing [Alexandra] Popova [his then girlfriend, now wife] to watch a video of the act. She also claimed that police super-glued stickers to her face and threatened to rape her. A clip later circulated on Telegram of the bruised and battered Kamardin apologising for his words.' Popova shouted 'Shame!' when the verdict was announced and was ushered out of the courtroom by bailiffs. 'It is a very harsh sentence. Seven years for poems, for a non-violent crime', she told the AFP news agency, before being taken away by police officers.

A lift on the horizon • The celebrated, beautiful Portico Library in Manchester proudly announced that it 'has been awarded a development grant by the National Lottery Heritage Fund to develop detailed plans to transform the unique historic library and secure its future by creating an accessible and sustainable space for arts, books, food, learning and history for Manchester's residents and visitors. Finally, a lift is on the horizon!' The process will take two years and may result in a transformation of one of the more iconic but neglected Victorian treasures of Manchester into a new kind of reading hub. 'There are lots of opportunities ahead and we're really looking forward to collaborating further, sharing ideas and working together to make the Portico a more accessible space – technically, creatively and intellectually.'

Het Onderwater Cabaret • Sonja Anderson reported in the *Smithsonian Magazine* (9 January) on Curt Bloch's almost invisible and very nearly erased editorial achievements in creating ninety-five issues of the satirical magazine *Het Onderwater Cabaret* while hiding from the Nazis in an attic. An exhibition of his little-known wartime publications is going on display in Berlin from February through May at the Jewish Museum in Berlin.

'For two years during World War II, a Jewish lawyer named Curt Bloch lived in an attic in the Netherlands, hiding from the Nazis. He received water, food and essentials from his hosts, as did thousands of other Jews hidden in similar circumstances. But Bloch's protectors also provided him with newspapers, pens, glue and other supplies. Each week, he used those materials to create a new issue of his own satirical magazine.' The title of the exhibition, *My Verses Are Like Dynamite*, is hardly an exaggeration in terms of the risks they took and the radical joy they must have provided their isolated readers. Anderson writes, 'Bloch's work was previously "almost completely unknown," as curator Aubrey Pomerance tells the *New York Times*' Nina Siegal. "The overwhelming majority of writings that were created in hiding were destroyed. If they weren't, they've come to the public attention before now. So, it's tremendously exciting."' In the mixture of irreverent art, poetry and song the issues open a row of vivid windows on a merciless period. The final issue of *Het Onderwater Cabaret* is dated 3 April 1945.

Reports

Report from Trinidad

The Twelve Days of Christmas

ANTHONY VAHNI CAPILDEO

This report comes to you from a little blue room of birds. The south wall consists of bookshelves above two built-in cupboards. An inbuilt gap in the middle allows the shelves to double as a desk. Nobody has used it as a desk. This report is being written on the Feast of the Holy Innocents. Warned by an angel, the Magi – the three wise men, astronomers 'of colour', as some would say now, more attentive to skin tone than aware of where on earth knowledge of the skies anciently was located – flee King Herod's land. They had meant well. They arrived with happy news of a kingly child. What a thing to tell a reigning king. Herod 'had all the male children killed who were two years old or under, reckoning by the date he had been careful to ask the wise men'. (Matthew 2:16, Jerusalem Bible). O trustful astronomers, who had not foreseen slaughter, when they gave the coordinates. My report's coordinates of place and time? Blue-infused, with birdcalls, on the fourth day of Christmas, 2023.

The 'twelve days of Christmas' run from 25 December onwards. 6 January is *el día de los Reyes*, the Day of the Kings. I cared less for their journey, than the excitement of counting. Where number failed was awesome. King Herod allegedly killing *all* the male children under the age of *two*: how? Checking a census? Searching all the nooks? How many is 'all'? The rabbits in Richard Adams's *Watership Down* can count up to four in Lapine, the language Adams invented for them. Anything more than four is *hrair*. If that children's book seems strangely bloodsoaked, that is not strange at all. Richard Adams based the fluffy critters' adventures on his service in the

Battle of Arnhem in 1944. War was not far from home. It just needed a little age-appropriate translation. King Herod arranged the state murder of *hrair* children.

For years I pondered *hrair*. So many! Never enough imagination! I loved counting: it bordered on the marvel and abyss of *hrair*. 'The Twelve Days of Christmas' became a favourite. This carol lists the gifts that someone's true love gives them on each day. Delightfully, it begins and ends with 'a partridge in a pear tree'. I was taught the perhaps false etymology for this phrase: a medieval mishearing of Latin, *apertuit in aperto*, meaning that she (the Virgin Mary) gave birth in the open. I was too young and foolish to care about maternal risk. I loved the plump creature nested high up in abundant foliage. What did the song promise, though? The daily gift of a partridge in a pear tree every day – items repeated, giving you hordes of things, people and creatures – or one-offs that added up? I'd be happy with one partridge.

Poets often make a living by creating educational materials that will train up more poets. Dear Reader, here is no homework, but five days' worth of poetical words, with inspirational quotations (at least, I like them).

1. Alphabet. Dictionaries may tell you that *alpha* and *beta* begin the Greek alphabet. Resemblance to letters in other, geographically contiguous alphabets is not coincidental. Dictionaries may not tell you this. 'Alphabet', formed of two letters, borrowed and compounded into a single word, means the whole set of letters. In 'After One Year', Martin Carter says:

> So jail me quickly, clang the illiterate door
> if freedom writes no happier alphabet.

On a recent work trip to San Francisco, I picked up Mosab Abu Toha's *Things You May Find Hidden in My Ear* (City Lights Book, 2022). This was before Israeli forces separated him from his wife and children while fleeing Gaza, and he began writing prose reports from a renewed ordeal. His début opens with 'Palestine A–Z', an abecedarian prose poem. Each letter is allotted two stanzas, with a gap, or border, axis of reflection, or breathing space, in between. Dear Reader, when reading aloud, where do you break, and how do you place pauses?

2. Gecko. Here in the little blue room of birds lives a gecko named Lorenzo. On the feast of the martyr St Laurence, he began chirruping responses to Spanish YouTube Mass. Since then, he seeks conversation with the humans in the household, and takes turns. Unbelievable? Locally, magic realism is pure realism... Once Lorenzo flattened, venturing behind the struts of the bookshelf. Like a lady sawn in half by a magician, part of him appeared either side of a piece of solid wood. Apparently divided, he emerged as whole. St Augustine, in his *Confessions* (tr. Henry Chadwick), writes:

> When I am sitting at home, a lizard catching flies or a spider entrapping them as they rush into its web often fascinates me. The problem is not made any different by the fact that the animals are small. The sight leads me on to praise you, the marvellous Creator and orderer of all things; but that was not how my attention first began.

The movement to praise reclaims a moment lost to distraction.

3. Beloved. *The Beloved Witness* (Viking, 1992) is the title of Jeet Thayil's selection of Kashmiri-American Agha Shahid Ali's poetry. It is also the name of the Agha Shahid Ali digital archive at Hamilton College in New York. Born in 1949 in New Delhi, dying in 2001 in Amherst, his unpretentious, wild, learned and moving art results from the fruitful encounter of European, Urdu, Arabic and Persian culture. Whoever encounters his work shares in this love, and in this witness. India's outrage to Kashmir is ongoing, as so many places to so many places; it is now a generation ago that the poet, imaginatively contemplating Srinagar's rubble, concludes 'The Country Without a Post Office'

> I've found a prisoner's letters to a lover –
> One begins: 'These words may never reach you.'
> Another ends: 'The skin dissolves in dew
> Without your touch. 'And I want to answer:
> I want to live forever. What else can I say?
> It rains as I write. Mad heart, be brave.

Shahid translates to 'witness' in Arabic and 'beloved' in Persian. There is a journey within that word, without boundary, without compounds. Aga Shahid Ali's final poem, 'The Veiled Suite', was a *canzone* that he had promised to the Israeli-American artist Izhar Patkin, and dictated to Patricia O'Neill, his friend and colleague; after his death, O'Neill would curate his archive at Hamilton. In Delhi, I heard Forrest Gander speak of him with great love. What would your archive consist of – tangible and intangible? Who would curate it? What fire would you take to it?

4. Pirate. If you can access the UK-based online Poetry Archive, you may enjoy listening to Jamaican genius Kei Miller (good son, good friend, good Carnival player) reciting 'How we became the pirates', in his unique, ex-preacherman voice.

> And what a thing to mock –
> the way we shape words differently.
> But maybe it's the old colonial hurt
> of how we became the pirates, dark people
> raiding English from the English,
> stealing poetry from the poets.

I am as guilty as anyone else of the occasional impulse to wear a ruffled shirt, but I know that folded into the word 'pirate' are many reversible ruffles of bleached and pleated theft.

5. Burn. How many libraries have been burnt over time? Why? In autumn 2023, I pleaded at the online AGM of the UK writers' registered trade union, the Society of Authors, for the deathly situation in Gaza to be addressed, as the deathly situation in Ukraine had been. I do not know how that organization, of which I am a member, may answer. A member... War, and genocide, target the spirit, in targeting the body. Enacting death to the letter, they burn to the ground the material foundations of a people's culture. Past, present and future then can be treated in terms of those tropes suspiciously popular in western culture: ghosts, ruins, traces. The Society of Authors, as far as I know, still campaigns against the Internet Archive, which offers free resources according to principles that seem to me library-like enough. I rely on it here in Trinidad, little provided with bookshops and libraries. I once wrote, in *Utter* (Peepal Tree, 2013):

Accept of me this staircase.
And that I too yearn skywards in the manifold increase
of simplicity for which there is another name.
And that we look up hotly.

Oh you are lifted from me!
And about that which I left
Unburnt

'Gift of a Staircase' was conceived as I stood among poet-friends on green grass in Delhi and heard about the devastation at Fukushima. The staircase itself reaches to the sky in an abandoned house in Port of Spain. The gift is hopeful. It invites you towards the *hrair* possibilities of a better world, *celeste*, *azur*.

Five days of words: enough to count on the fingers of one hand (if you're lucky to have a full set of them). Do you want twelve words, to make up the carol? There remains a week's worth of lexical items, and literary snippets, to fill in, illustrate, ponder in your heart, or sing. What will yours be?

Eddie Linden 1935–2023

HILARY DAVIES

The death of the publisher and poet Eddie Linden, aged eighty-eight, marks the passing of one of the most distinctive figures in post-war British poetry. Passionate literary advocate, formidable networker, vehement socialist, conflicted Catholic, vociferous homosexual, obstreperous friend – for nearly fifty years this indomitable bundle of contradictions was a presence on the poetry scene in London, in Dublin, in Edinburgh, in Glasgow.

Yet who was Eddie Linden? The story of his childhood and upbringing is well known, not only from Sebastian Barker's biography of him, *Who is Eddie Linden* (Jay Landesman, 1971), but from Eddie himself, who was infamous for buttonholing strangers over a drink to relate who he was. Or who he had constructed himself to be. Such moments are beautifully captured in Gerald Mangan's affectionate cartoon of Eddie, published in the festschrift in honour of his eightieth birthday, *Eddie's Own Aquarius,* in which an enquiring Eddie looks up at a distinctly gruff God the Father while the archangel Gabriel nervously explains, 'He says he's a manic-depressive alcoholic lapsed-Catholic Irish working-class pacifist-communist bastard from Glasgow. And would you like to subscribe to a poetry magazine?'

That's the legend. And of course in part the reality. The key to this legend is the poetry magazine, *Aquarius.* Until the age of thirty, Eddie led a life that can genuinely be described as picaresque, witness the definition here which could have been written of and for Eddie, '*pícaro*: the outcast who attempts to survive precariously within a hostile environment... the *pícaro*... devises pragmatic strategies of survival... not an outright rebel, but self-interestedly pragmatic and ready to do whatever it takes to survive on a daily basis.'

Born illegitimate to poor Catholic parents in an era when such an event brought down opprobrium and shame, Eddie grew up in the 1930s and 1940s as an unwanted foster child in Belshill, a working-class outlier of Glasgow. These were tough times and places, and Eddie was seriously disadvantaged even within that context. His education was skimpy and he never learnt to write fluently, although reading was a different matter: he was a classic autodidact and also a classic 'foundling' child, always looking for security and identity. He was restless too, with a succession of low-paid manual jobs, as a steel worker, miner (for which he was deemed not strong enough), British Rail porter; and a succession of lodgings, shifting constantly between Motherwell, Corby, where he had an uncle, and the seedier districts of London. And yet.

In his early adulthood Eddie identified with Communism as a substitute for the Catholic Church which for a time he felt had rejected him but which he never entirely rejected. Father Anthony Ross, whom he met at Laxton Hall near Corby, was an important influence in enabling Eddie to address the tensions between his homosexuality and his Catholic upbringing. Eddie went on to help found Catholic CND, with whom he went on the Aldermaston marches, and the Simon Community for the homeless in East London.

It was through gay friendships in London that he met John Heath-Stubbs and his circle, and through friends in the Catholic Labour movement that he eventually got a place at Plater College, Oxford, founded to offer education to people precisely like Eddie. Although he very quickly abandoned formal study, while in the city he did meet Roger Garfitt and the young poets Craig Raine and Sebastian Barker, son of George Barker and Elizabeth Smart and Eddie's future biographer. It was a short step to the Colony Room and the bohemian atmosphere of Soho in the 1960s, not perhaps in its heyday but still very active. Soon Eddie was attending poetry readings, and, one day, he had the idea of publishing these poets himself.

This was the turning point. Harold Pinter helped with money, the name *Aquarius* was chosen (the musical *Hair,* with its trademark opening song, 'The Age of Aquarius', had just opened in London) and, because of the friendships Eddie had established, he was uniquely well placed to call on famous contributors, but also spot up-and-coming talent. The first issue, which appeared in 1969, contained work by the young Frances Horovitz, Kevin Crossley-Holland, Libbie Houston, Dinah Livingstone and Anthony Howell, as well as Thomas Blackburn and Michael Horovitz, the latter already an enfant terrible of new British poetry after his Children of Albion event at the Albert Hall in 1965. This was soon followed by numbers that included work by Paul Muldoon, Paul Durcan and Barry MacSweeney, all still in their early twenties; other writers at the start of their careers were Seamus Heaney, Eiléan Ní Chuilleanáin, Peter Fallon (still a teenager) and Michael Hartnett; the Scottish poets Stewart Conn, Tom Leonard and Alan Bold; from Wales Meic Stephens, Gillian Clarke and Ruth Bidgood. To these we must add those already established – although in his verbal expostulations, Eddie himself could be fiercely partisan, the names I cite here are chosen to give a sense of the huge range of poets, poetic styles and affiliations that Eddie published, and this over several poetic generations: Elizabeth Jennings, Fred Grubb, John Montague, Norman Nicholson, Sidney Goodsir Smith, Kit Wright, Brian Patten, R.S. Thomas, Norman MacCaig, Ted Hughes, Maureen Duffy and Helen Dunmore. It's an astonishing and far from exhaustive roster.

In latter years Eddie used guest editors with special issues devoted to Canadian, Australian and women's writing, in addition to celebratory numbers for John Heath-Stubbs, George Barker, W.S. Graham and Roy Fuller. He became a stalwart, and outspoken, member of the general council of the Poetry Society, being especially active in promoting the move of the organization from Earl's Court to Covent Garden, a move that was not without controversy but which ensured the long-term survival and health of the Society today.

Personally, Eddie was a loyal and generous friend who promoted other writers' talents selflessly: yes, he could be infuriating and embarrassing at times, but he worked tirelessly for the good of poetry in Britain for nearly fifty years. We are all the poorer for his going.

Set 2: Mondo de Mašino

TRANSLATED BY JOHN GALLAS

1
Cablecars *Shigeji Tsuboi 1897–1975/Japan*

Way way down, under beetling crags,
a quick, pinched river, startling blue, busies on.
Way way above, in the unmargined sky,
the cablecars move along in quiet order.
The heavy wire, invisible with air,
conducts with patient power
its hushed, believing loads
across the gap of Time. I think –
unsnapped so far – I too hold something
that goes on, and seems to work.

2
Worldsend *Jakob van Hoddis 1887–1942/Jewish Germany*

Mr Normal's hat flies off his head,
What should be nice fresh air goes *eek* and *thud,*
Roofers fall off rooves and fall down dead,
And round the coast (*it says*) it's flood, flood, flood.

The wind is up, a mad sea storms the Drains
And crushes all the Dams and Overflows.
Everyone has coughs and colds, and trains
Fall off the railway bridges. So it goes.

3
Untitled *Sa'di 1210–91/2/Persia*

In out, in out, these breaths, being the count
of love, are each worth the time they take.
I pass the night in expectation of day.
That is hardly new. Except it is your face.
I long to see you again: you who are
less faithful and less often than the planets.

Thud thud, this heart is strong enough
to bear it. You made it so to tire it out so well.
They can say what they like: I don't care.
The wheel goes round. Winter turns into Spring.
Layla took Majnun for his mad desire.
My caution too has turned to fire. I love you.
A little tame dove you need no rope to keep.

I am strong with lack of sleep. And lack of hope.
One is past and the other will not come.
Let them go. These seconds and these breaths,
the old insistent heart: keep me alive.

4
Smalltown Yala *Anonymous 20th century/Kenya*

Yala, this song's for you, Yala, your song –
O O O O

O all the little accountants are scribbling scribbling here
very busy here very very busy here

O Adoray's dress is flowers on the outside here
and plain here on the inside here

O Amara's mum can't afford a bike here
so she walks here and there here

O the Kamnaras bowl round on bikes here
there here and everywhere here

O Oloo Nyabondo drummer has given up trains here
he's so busy here so very busy here

O will they let Oloo drummer on a plane there
it's so busy there so very busy there

Yala, this one's for you, Yala, your song O O O –
with your little accountants scribbling scribbling

5
The Steam Chopper *Guiseppe Giusti 1809–50/Italy*

In China there's this steam machine
that drives a guillotine
in three hours it can shift 100,000 heads in a row
in one go.

Everyone's talking about it. The Holy Thingummies can see
that the whole country
will be Civilized pretty soon, and make the Eurocrats
look like twats.

His Sublime Cloudiness is an Honourable Man: a bit nasty and tight,
a bit thick, but a real Benthamite,
and a Father to His People and happy to patronize whatever
looks Arty or Clever.

Some dumb, ungrateful tribe of his refused to pay
their Phase 2 Tax and Import Duty Section A,
so his Sublime Benevolence sent the Thing to persuade
them. They paid.

The Chief Chopper is famous and rich, with a Huge Pension
in honour of his Invention,
and Patent Payments and Prizes and Promotions, and spends his time shopping
In Beijing.

The Holy Brothers say they're keen to get him baptised quick,
and the tinpot Duke of Modena says to his sidekick:
O O O why don't such a super Social Pioneer
live round here?

*

Acknowledgements
1. Tsuboi – new translation
2. Hoddis – new
3. Sa'di – new
4. Kenya – from *The Song Atlas* (lineation altered)
5. Giusti – from *52 Euros* (lineation altered)

Letter from Wales

SAM ADAMS

Occasionally, glancing idly at books on shelves, we are shaken by sombre reflections. In this way, and with just such a jolt, I recently came across a collection of poems entitled *3 Young Anglo-Welsh Poets*, published by the Welsh Arts Council in January 1974. It would have been remarkable at the time if only because grants from the Council's Literature Committee for the making and selling of books were intended to be handed out to established Welsh publishers. I can imagine Meic Stephens, then WAC Literature Director, arguing forcibly, from his great height, that since the book was the outcome of the Council's 1973 'Young Poets Competition' it was entirely appropriate the Council should publish it. There were probably protests from the publishing sector, but I don't recall them now. What I do remember is that judging the competition was difficult. Of course, the intention had been to select an outright winner, but when that proved impossible, the only solution was to share the prize. So it came about that this slim volume (thirty poems in all) launched three new, distinctive poetic voices: Duncan Bush, Tony Curtis and Nigel Jenkins. Looking back, I would still argue that the tripartite division of the prize was a good decision. All three subsequently gained distinction, and further Arts Council prizes, as writers of both poetry and prose, and in December 1998, there was a late celebration of sorts, when they were brought together again for a reading at Blackwood Miners' Institute in the Gwent valleys. It was a splendid, well-attended evening, and as we wrapped things up the poets signed my copy of the book they share, one with a note saying, 'thanks, twenty-five years later, for the prize. *Dymuniadau cynnes*'. With the added Welsh warmth of good wishes, that was, typically, Nigel Jenkins. Now, another twenty-five years down the line, we can celebrate the publication of *Wild Cherry* (Parthian), his selected poems, edited by Patrick McGuinness, whose introductory essay praises the poetry as essentially public utterance, quoting from a talk by the poet in 1995: 'Poetry should be out and about, doing a job in the world, ambushing people, not hiding in classroom cupboards and magazines that nobody reads'. Nigel Jenkins practised what he preached.

He had, for a Welshman, an unusual early life. Born in 1949 at Gorseinon in industrial south-west Wales and brought up on a farm on the Gower peninsula, he had a public school education, which, one might suppose, gave him both a desire to break away and the confidence to do so. He was at various times reporter for a newspaper in Leamington Spa, circus-hand in the USA and wanderer in Europe and North Africa, before taking up a place at Essex University to study comparative literature and film. We are told he returned to his home patch in 1976, having already committed himself to learning the Welsh language and writing. He married and settled in Mumbles, a village on the headland a few miles west of Swansea city centre, and close to his Gower roots.

He was sturdy, black-bearded, wore a broad-brimmed hat and boots – and, indeed, sat a horse well. There was something about the man, his easy manner and fine voice, that drew others to him. He was a genuinely popular writer, even among those who have little time for literature. Yet recognition might have been restricted to Wales and, curiously you may think, to people of the Khasi Hills in north-east India converted to Christianity by Welsh missionaries, about whom he wrote *Gwalia in Khasia* (Gomer, 1995, and Wales Book of the Year 1996), were it not for the notoriety of his 'Execrably Tasteless Farewell to Viscount No'. This was a poem on the death of Speaker George Thomas (who had said 'No' to Welsh devolution), that was published prominently in the *Guardian* in 1997. In poems like that and the anti-militarist 'Warhead' he upheld the ancient Welsh tradition of the poet as social commentator and, if he has his way, influencer. Nor did he stop at versifying: a CND activist and disarmament protester, he went to gaol rather than pay a fine.

Farming and the Gower inevitably find a place in earlier poems in this selection. The farmyard scene, rusting implements, thrashing, the slaughtering of a pig, the castrating of a bull calf, and the stallion in 'Stud', 'addict, professional', moving 'stiff-legged' to the waiting mare, all bear witness to hands-on familiarity with rural life. At home, too, with his grandmother, he encountered Welsh as a living language and laid the foundation of the facility he acquired later, along with the bitter irony of 'Land of Song: i.m. 1.iii.79' – the date of the first Welsh poll, which rejected devolution:

Sing with the blinding *hwyl*
Of it all: you are programmed
to sing: England expects –
my hen laid a haddock
and all that stuff.

'Never Forget Your Welsh' is a blistering collection of newspaper-style headlines on the manifold ills of Wales playing upon a familiar beer advertisement with a background threnody of lines from the sixth-century 'Y Gododdin', which tells of the disastrous defeat of the Welsh-speaking men of the north at the hands of the invading Angles.

Jenkins's personality lives in the poems – robust, sure-footed, yet haunted by the vicissitudes and cruelties of life. His instinct is to see things as they are, tell truth. 'Forty-Eight and a Half', a poem about his father, begins 'Here I am, Dad, this is the month / I overtake you...',

Foxhunting Taff with a penchant for the shires,
you had your Scotch and Three Nuns, your loud afraid
laughter

warmed a place you were public schooled not to
understand...
... the dreamplate
departed Mum's hand, missed your head and broke
a family's heart: too much horseflesh, too little love.

The poetry shirks nothing and illuminates a great deal, from the essentially playful sequence of 'Punctuation Poems' to the intensely personal, and salvos inspired by contemporary public life. In the early 'from the Triads' he borrowed the medieval poetic formula to make caustic fun at the expense of contemporary figures and politics, and a good deal of his later poetry has the character of gnomic utterance, terse and sharp or concisely reflective, as in 'A Body of Questions':

Is happiness simply the absence of pain?

Is hell the pain
we know we cause others?

It was an inspired choice (by Meic) that Nigel was commissioned to write the volume on John Tripp in the Writers of Wales series, which turned out to be one of its highlights. Patrick McGuinness's introduction notes his kinship with both Tripp and Harri Webb. He certainly shared with them elements of a common outlook on politics and life, but was very much his own man in person and the range, nature and style of his writing.

The publication of *Wild Cherry* is a reminder of the range and quality of Nigel Jenkins's poetic output. He was in addition a playwright, a psychogeographer and editor of the English-language version of the *Encyclopaedia of Wales* (2008). He died in 2014, with much more still to do and say. Duncan Bush, another of the '3 Young Anglo-Welsh Poets', who won Wales Book of the Year in 1995 for his poetry collection *Masks* and was also novelist and translator, died in 2017.

The City, an Argument

JAMES WOMACK

I.

Beloved, the city curves as a sickle. Politicians have written rhapsodies to its impermanence, its occasional gross expansions. Month on month the city drags the sea close into its formal harbours and casual inlets. An odd kind of embrace followed soon after by predictable rejection. The walls do not yield.

Beloved, the city does not stay still. Where was wasteland a month ago now a suburb: uninhabited, pristine, bright. The arterial roads mirage from the sun. The direction of travel is not yet determined. Running to or running away. A liquid, it fills all available space. Alleyways writhe and cross.

Beloved, the city knows its worth. No traveller comes here but is informed of this fact. Chauvinism shades into a kind of weeping arrogance. Microcosm, every barrio believes itself better than the others. After the match each weekend there is always violence. This is not unusual. A boy is stabbed.

Beloved, the city is still a child. Incontinent, satisfied with a breast and a swaddled bed. Useless from labour. Useless for work. The city *does* nothing: it takes and grows. The city has your eyes. We look at the city with the love we cannot spare for our own children.

Beloved, the city is sexless. The ripe displays of our childhood have disappeared. A new louder kind of innocence. Mystics and stylites have a vocabulary we cannot coincide. Vows are asked of them. To flee in a desert the approach of mankind. The city asks no new vows of us.

Beloved, in a mirror the city confuses us. We never invited mirror trust. It seems a test of some kind. To have your own face given back to you upside-down. Your teeth where your windows should be. Roads instead of the tight squirms and curls of a more legitimate brain.

Beloved, the city wakes up after the weekend. The city is in the corner of your eye. You hope that some fragment of the dead days will survive. An abandoned high-heel shoe. An abandoned pint glass of shocking orange urine. Full of commuters an abandoned train passes over a bridge.

II.

Beloved, the city is nothing if not just. A single glance, the wrong word at the wrong time means honour must be satisfied. Duels, rapier or pistol, take place on the dusty backlots. When the city is called to join our larger wars, then all personal affronts are temporarily abandoned.

Beloved, the city splits and runs like a silver ball. Touched it does nothing other than yield, for all that we wish it to resist. In the harshest winters it moves sluggishly. In high summer it hurtles around like a mad thing, separating and resolving into grand bridges and towers.

Beloved, the city makes great claims for its intellect. Coupled with a certain moral flexibility, this has led to its current line of work. The machine works slowly but is always effective. Shipping movements are relayed to its superiors. Blood bubbles out and drips from the side of its head.

Beloved, the city feeds itself. It can nourish itself on perfumes – road tar and frying fish, the sweat and Chanel of summer – as well as the more recognisable steaks and garbage. Roles forced upon us. We are à la carte anatomists. This is not just food. It is unjust food.

Beloved, there are times when the city is generous. The tables spread to groaning. The mother runs unchallenged from the corner shop, her child both shield and excuse of the tins stashed under the pushchair. Pavements split with dandelions, purslane. Feast at the corner where dogs piss. Burdock and bedstraw.

Beloved, the city can never say it is sated. Ephemera we think we lose are never fully vanished. The scroll of a price tag picked off and rolled away. The playing cards spilled from a window. Flirtatious auto-destruct online messages. The city gathers it all, the city always wants more.

Beloved, the city shows its morning face. That noise the grim of adolescent complaint, the background hum of everything not being perfect. Shells and slime! Move it, move it! A step slower than our slowest participant. Industrial concrete suddenly an object of deep interest. The end of it an education.

III.

Beloved, a city for lovers. Lovers congregate at sites of least offensive photographic interest. Bridges collapse under the weight of padlocks. A single man cannot move from the hospital to the churchyard unless he elbow himself past crowds of the infatuated. Buses arrive daily on swift turnarounds. Open for business.

Beloved, the city is an undelivered city of messengers. News is borne from the northern hills to the curve of the central river, in the movement of an eye and the turn of a hand. All is information, messages transmitted and eternally received. A letter always arrives at its destination.

Beloved, your city is an angry city. Peevish even before the morning fog has been burned away, we notice the first signs in earbud executives, their wasp-sharp faces. One spark could set the Whole. Thing. Off. A man jostled at the wrong moment, a car changing lanes. Don't touch me!

Beloved, the city is a clamshell on the waves. There was land, and then there was hell, and then there was the eternal city. Born naked. It drives you mad, the city, that itch at the edge of your waking mind. No way but this. When desire fades, you weep.

Beloved, the city can restrain itself. Gourmet and not gourmand, we are invited to know the city as a set of experiences, of visits to the planetarium, the pumping station, the light on the sandy college walls, wondering if here, here will be a first kiss, a first brief declaration.

Beloved, this week's monster is the city. Baleen-mouthed, it battens on the excreta of its parasites, our abandoned residue, gorging itself on grease and turds, wet-wipes and condoms, slow water and the unbearable rush of the tunnel bore. You know this sick greed, the squabble to consume, vomit, consume again.

Beloved, the city eats and shits its citizens. One glorious morning! Our impedimenta tied in a handkerchief, stick slung over our shoulder, we arrive and see the skyline awaken before us in its watercolour gold. No illusion can hold this back: each tower is hard enamel, mouth whole, tongue river.

IV.

Beloved, the city is always upwards. Complaints no longer reach the tops of the tallest buildings. The skyline that so impressed our ancestors is seen now as prelude. The future tall, a ladder to the moon. Glass and steel hacked from the Welsh mines, dragged overland at immense human cost.

Beloved, the city blows a trumpet. Boots and saddles. Drop everything and prepare for war. There on the coast the enemy hordes, weapons concealed in torn canvas bags, their uniform ragged, their pockets empty, most of them dead. The survivors disguised as women and children. As expected, we shall resist.

Beloved, the city this morning looks cruel. Her lip a harsh slash of Rouge Diabolique, her eyes defined into oblivion. Sometimes one dresses to impress, sometimes one must dress to intimidate. Makeup is an environment. Even the clouds seem to catch themselves and redress. Even the clouds, even the rain.

Beloved, the city is a noted carouser. Drink so deep from the ramshorn that the seas sink and drowned villages rise above the waves. Eat so greedily that the plates themselves are consumed. Relax with one final sherry in the Senior Common Room, the World Serpent purring at your feet.

Beloved, the city is an ant-nest miracle. From the gritted outyards to the nucleus, that black hole which drags everything – mostly money – into its orbit, each eusocial part seems to work for the good of the whole. What a fine place to sink into, one might think, sinking irreparably in.

Beloved, there are no other cities. None at least that compare with this one. The hamlets and hovels which surround us can only dream of their submission or incorporation. The height of yearning, to be one day suburbia. Parkway. Golf course. What we are owed is only what we deserve.

Beloved, there is no way to look directly at the city. Spend too long with your eyes open, and you will no longer see colours. All will fade to a forgetful grey, and the soft faces of those who walk towards you will seem indeterminate, the faces of the dead.

V.

Beloved, the city just wants to be touched, or believes it wants to be touched. Although, if it is touched, the slightest contact will snail it back into its home. It is easy to offend the city. Imagined slights become vast bubbles. I thought you were such a good friend.

Beloved, the city has been caught *in flagrante*, its dick in the pie. You can understand the temptation, but such invitations should be resisted. The chiselled boulevards, the air and delicacy of the parks, all swaying together in a single inescapable net. The rest of the pantheon invited to mock.

Beloved, is the city implacable? Are we no more than some great Bedlam, where our crimes are on display alongside our foibles, and the gross public uses us as a Sunday afternoon excursion? Is the Casa Mila a source of innocent merriment? Is there balance, or justice? Is there sickness?

Beloved, the city invites us to pursue her, right to the doors of her many bedchambers. A question, in this brave world of questions: when is the right moment to abandon the chase? Our deserts, the gratification of these desires – the city turns to us and never seems so beautiful.

Beloved, the city knows empathy can be fatal. Is there anything worse than the way certain stories end? I know what you're going through. Come, sit next to me. Poor child. There is manipulation in the city's kindness, just as there can be a degree of innocence in her anger.

Beloved, the city reaches into the ricebowl with almost delicate fingers. Sorts the grain from the maggots, divides what will be left from what is to be consumed. A handful of that writhing protein, that gives you soul in your mouth. Void heart. King soul. Our customs are not yours.

Beloved, the end of the city is upon us. The sharp shadow decadence that overcomes her every seven days. 'This is a kind of marriage,' we once thought, equating partnership with surrender. A two days' wonder. The blurred head of the morning after; the life of the world to come.

VI.

Beloved, the city only sometimes hurries to life. Crowds gather like sunspots at the naos. A hundred myriad people, men and boys, follow the swings and cycles. I lived close to this temple once, and could hear nothing from my lover's shuttered window. This does not mean that nothing happened.

Beloved, the city low-key flicks v-signs at hearses. A family of ten children is common and supported by the state. Everyone will live forever is the general tenor of things. The Year 6 Parents WhatsApp group is the place to hunt for resources: flat-front grey cotton trousers; a solid-state orthicon.

Beloved, the city doesn't want to hear this. Furious mothers calling their children home in the mid-afternoon, the siesta ruptured, the panic setting in to their voices. All the children hurried in from the streets, the parks left in the burning sun, an ice-cream van calling uselessly across the tarmac.

Beloved, in the hills around the city a storm has flourished for the past three and a half centuries. Travellers speak of dust clouds and an intense suffocating heat, something under the ground that groans and curses. A space of withered trees and abandoned settlements it is impolite to discuss.

Beloved, the city is a trapdoor spider. That tribe which Walckenaer has named *vagrants*. From a little cell formed of the rolled up leaf of a plant, it darts upon any insect which happens to pass. The city and its affinities conceal themselves in a long cylindrical straight silken tube.

Beloved, there is a knock at the city gate. Feet shuffle towards the barred wooden wicket. The peephole – it is late at night – swings open, with a faint yellow light behind it. The lockkeeper voice that asks your business is querulous, ancient. For an old man to have such power.

Beloved, the city is hungry, hungry beyond need. It eats what it wants, and whatever it does not want. Touch it: the city will have you in its mouth forever. You are not entrapped to your return: instead – all the better to eat you with – it's love that calls you.

VII.

Beloved, the city will do nothing. I passed one of its gardens, and saw the wild roses grow, the thorn and the unkempt thistle spread and stretch. It tells you its dreams, and talks of food and drink: an animal life. Laziness by what authority? The city has no scripture.

Beloved, the city opens and breathes. You can say to yourself 'Well I give what I give'; the relationship is always uneven. Saints and ascetics are donors above us, but net recipients even they. Six o'clock in the afternoon approaches: what have we done to earn this calm, these bells?

Beloved, the city has been petulant, has soldiered, has set itself above us all. And what of it? Now she is small and new-unknowledged, curled asleep on a beanbag. Her face has relaxed into the speaking mask of all children; as a mind builds behind it, and all we owe.

Beloved, the city invites us to this square. Walk the length of one side: the sheltered one. Perfumeries and sweet shops. Quarter turn. Walk, *pausadamente*. Quarter turn. Walk, exhaling. High-end boutiques and hat stalls. Quarter turn. *Pausadamente*, again. You are both where you began, and five hundred yards further on.

Beloved, the city of all things is the smallest. A nothing in permanent harsh light. To look at, barely more than a grain, subdued and uncommunicative. The Tsar once offered a prize to anyone who could measure the city, a prize which remained unclaimed at the time of his death.

Beloved, there remains one barrier to victory over the city. Anti-climb paint and cacti spikes. Every day more people make the attempt. I saw wounds to hands and feet, the side, the head. I saw one arm, skin split like a torsioning weisswurst; its owner a mute and dazed fourteen-year-old.

Beloved, there is a softening in the city. Grey hair forms rings around her head, around his head (for what pronouns the city has!). This skin has survived intact, and is now soft as shammy-leather. Strange and expensive ointments, applied daily, over the course of several lustra. You may touch.

VIII.

Tenella! Tenella! Tenella!
Tenella! Tenella! Tenella!

Beloved, the city is mine now. That throb at the back of your head – my feet, dancing. Let us not say I come from the east, the south: let us instead say only I am here from *elsewhere*. But you know me, do you not? Cousin, you do know me?

1939: Before Darkness Fell*

IAN THOMSON

'No one knew that this was to be the infamous year of the Munich Pact, but everyone knew that soon there would be a new world war...'

Delmore Schwartz, 'New Year's Eve'

Erich Haugas and his sisters Benita and Ella

In the summer of 1939 my grandfather Erich Haugas took part in an international agricultural conference in Budapest. He was thirty-eight and his professional pride was flattered. As a chemist he was in charge of the Dairy Export Control Station laboratory in the Estonian capital of Tallinn. To his untravelled eyes this was the trip of a lifetime: Budapest was the last stretch of Western 'civilization' before the East and the closest to a West European capital many Estonians would ever get. No direct train went to Hungary: Erich had to take three trains through Latvia, Polish-occupied Lithuania, Poland and the Nazi vassal state of Slovakia: a round trip of 2,300 miles across European frontiers electric with future troubles. The fear of world war was in many minds all over Europe – but to my grandfather the rumours of war were just that: rumours.

His wife Elfriede was anxious. There was no sane reason Erich had to go: a number of delegates had turned down invitations. The calamity of Poland was close at hand but if Erich sensed the gathering emergency, he did not let it show. With a suitcase packed for a two-week absence he arrived at the Baltic Station in the early hours of a July morning. The Tallinn platform was buzzing with the excitement of an imminent departure. The Estonian State Railways express to Budapest was made up of smart dark green carriages, and in the restaurant car the tables lit by small lamps were already laid for breakfast. The purser showed my grandfather to the compartment he was to share with the Estonian journalist Artur Taska, who was due to get on at the Polish–Slovak border. Prominent figures in Estonian public life – agronomists, writers, politicians – were on the train bound for Budapest, among them Estonia's military attaché to Hungary, Ludvig Jakobsen, and the opera soprano Milvi Laid. Heinrich Feischner, the classical composer, had a sleeping-berth to himself (his father owned the ritzy Café Feischner in Tallinn). In the first-class couchettes a group of agricultural commercial advisers were busy discussing wheat husking and milk powder manufacture. Velda Aurora Rüütli, a platinum-blonde orthodontist attached to Budapest University, sat on her own in a compartment adjacent to them; she was the kind of Estonian woman who could take care of herself. Horticulturalists from Helsinki, hoping to enjoy a summer holiday in Budapest with their wives, wore light linen 'sporting' suits and straw sun boaters. Up the aisle the porters came carrying hat boxes and trunks. Voices reached my grandfather in his compartment. 'Are you travelling to Budapest?' 'No, not so far – only to Riga.' Baron Vladimir Bulgarin, a Baltic German chemist, was travelling to Brno University in Nazi-annexed Moravia. Already there was an atmosphere on board of Alfred Hitchcock's 1938 railway thriller *The Lady Vanishes.*

The station clock struck the hour – 9am – and the train began to move. On the platform Elfriede raised a hand in farewell – and then she was gone. The train settled to its rhythm and soon it was racing over the rails. Outside Jäneda the trackway broadened and the signals flashed green across the stations: Tapa, Jõgeva, Tabivere. My grandfather was still at breakfast when the express reached the Estonian university town of Tartu (where, in 1901, he had been born to a minor Tsarist functionary). The July sun fell on Tartu's wood-and-glass railway station and on the viaduct bridge at Elva beyond. At Valga four hours later the train came to a halt. Valga was on the Estonian–Latvian border and rife with smuggling. On the Latvian side the station was called Valka. ('One Town, Two Countries', people joked.) The small dusty Estonian station had VALGA painted in black letters on the customs shed.

Estonian frontier police in grey fatigues came down between the lines with leashed dogs. They made a list of all the passengers on the train – names, nationalities – and examined passports and exit visas and searched everyone's luggage. Among those who got on at Valga was the Finnish music prodigy Heikki Lahti; soon there would not be a town of any size between Riga and Prague where the six-year-old mandolin virtuoso had not performed. Lahti was travelling to Budapest with the Estonian theatre director Jullo Talpsepp as his chaperone. A number of Polish and Lithuanian nationals boarded. Szepsel Berkman, an accountant, was on his way to visit Jewish relatives in Vilnius in Polish Lithuania. Jews were not popular. The only head of state at this time to extend a helping hand to Jews was General Rafael Trujillo of the Dominican Republic; by issuing Jews with 100,000 visas he hoped to increase the 'white' population of his Carib-

* *1939: Before Darkness Fell* is an essay from a work-in-progress. The idea for it grew out of a piece on Eric Ambler by Ian Thomson which was originally published in *Slightly Foxed*.

bean country, which was mostly mixed-race or black.* In the end only a few hundred Jews – Austrian, Polish, German – settled in Trujillo's Caribbean haven. Admiral Horthy, the antisemitic and anti-Slav regent of Hungary, had allied himself with Hitler in the hope of reclaiming lands lost to Hungary after the First World War. With the Führer's help Horthy had already recovered parts of southern Slovakia and Subcarpathian Ruth (the birthplace in 1892 of Andy Warhol's mother Julia Warhola). European power politics in the late Thirties were a dirty game played out by the dictators.

Belching steam, the train edged backwards out of Valga through a level-crossing. The Latvian border – a stretch of no man's land called the 'Neutral Zone' – was closed off by a barrier of carmine red and white, the Latvian colours. An official with the Red Lion and Silver Griffin of Latvia on his cap banged down a VALKAS STACIJĀ (Valka Station) stamp on my grandfather's passport and three hours later the train pulled into the Latvian capital of Riga. More Budapest congress delegates got on at Riga. Columns of steam rose from the waiting engine while porters loaded the guard's van with crates of food and alcohol. From Riga the train continued on to Daugavpils (Dvinsk under the Tsars). Daugavpils had a rich Jewish culture – the American painter Mark Rothko was born there in 1903 – but the station would soon facilitate the industrial horror that was Hitler's war on Polish Jewry: Daugavpils was a key junction for trains coming in from Jewish-populated Warsaw and Vilnius.

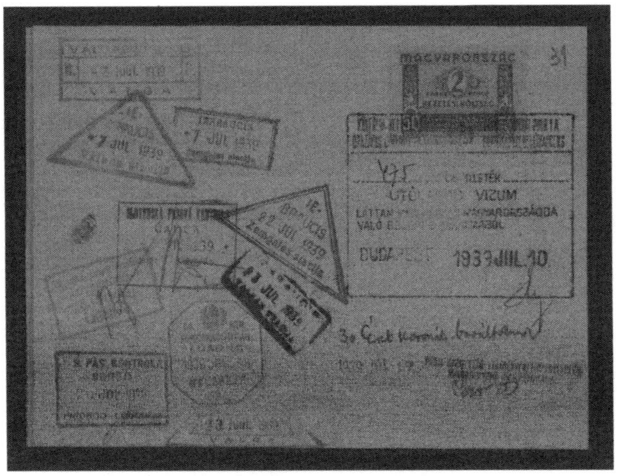

Erich Haugas: visa stamps

Before long the train had reached Zemgale, the border point between southern Latvia and Poland. Built in 1922, Zemgale station today serves as a Roman Catholic church but in my grandfather's day it was a vital crossroads – Latvia's gateway into Central and Southern Europe. Inevitably Zemgale stood on contested lands. In 1920, after seizing a sliver of Lithuania, Poland had claimed part of Latvia's border close to Zemgale. Violence was mounting daily in Polish-annexed central Lithuania between Polish and Lithuanian nationals. The train lurched and the points changed before it reached the Polish border station of Turmonolo (now Turmantas in Lithuania), a main transit point for Kharkiv in Soviet Ukraine on the Tsarist-era Warsaw–St Petersburg line. Armed with revolvers, Polish customs control got on the train and asked to see identification papers.

Next stop was Vilnius, the de jure capital of Lithuania, which Lithuania had surrendered to Poland in 1922 following the Polish-Lithuanian conflict that broke out after the First World War (Vilnius was 'Wilno' to the Poles). The train continued along the Katowice line across western Belarus to arrive at Bialystok, the largest city in north-eastern Poland, situated now in the so-called Suwalki Gap, a sixty-mile-long strip of Poland and Lithuania straddled to the west by Putin's Russia and to the east by Belarus under Putin's dictator ally Lukashenko. If there is to be a Third World War, say the experts, it may flare up here.

Soon Warsaw approached and in their sleeping cars the passengers stirred. The gold watch in my grandfather's nightshirt pocket – his father Johannes Haugas's gold watch in its dented case – kept time but what time was it? A mass of blast furnaces and ancient castles rose along the line. At Warsaw Central the passengers got off and changed trains. The new train would go all the way to Athens via Istanbul. During the three-hour wait that morning my grandfather had time to enquire at the newly opened Slovak embassy in Warsaw if visas were required of Estonian nationals. The embassy said they were not: as a newborn republic, Slovakia felt a kinship with the twenty-year-old Estonia.

On 8 July – day two of my grandfather's journey across the disputed lands of pre-war Europe – the frontiers of Poland and Slovakia converged at the Polish station of Czaca on the edge of the Nazi-occupied Czech territories. Depending on whether the speaker was Polish, Magyar, Czech or Slovak, the railway station was Czaca, Czadca, Čaca or Čadca (the diacritic over the C created an unmistakably Slovakian 'tch' sound.) The station buffet, with its filigree gables and Alpine-style window-boxes, served Polish beer in silver-lidded tankards. Strikingly, the two Polish borders Erich Haugas had crossed thus far – at Zemgale and Czaca – were the result of inter-war nationalist annexations. In autumn 1938 Poland had grabbed a part of Slovakia close to Czaca, an annexation of Czech-governed territory that amounted to an attack on fellow Slavs and appeared to put Warsaw on the same low moral level as Nazi Berlin. The Polish government was now actively pursuing right-wing antisemitic policies of varying toxicity and had orchestrated a campaign of 'Polonisation' that exalted the Catholic Polish race and nation over Russian territorial expansionist ambitions. There were now 'ghetto benches' in Polish universities, with quotas restricting the number of Jews able to graduate.

* Trujillo's contempt for the 'backward and dirty' Vodou-ridden black immigrant workers from neighbouring Haiti led, in October 1937, to a massacre on the Dominican sugar plantations of some 25,000 Haitian cane-cutters. The racialist purge was reported in the Estonian press; Trujillonian ethnic cleansing – to use that horrible term – provided a template for Hitler's imminent ethnocides and racial 'solutions'.

Artur Taska

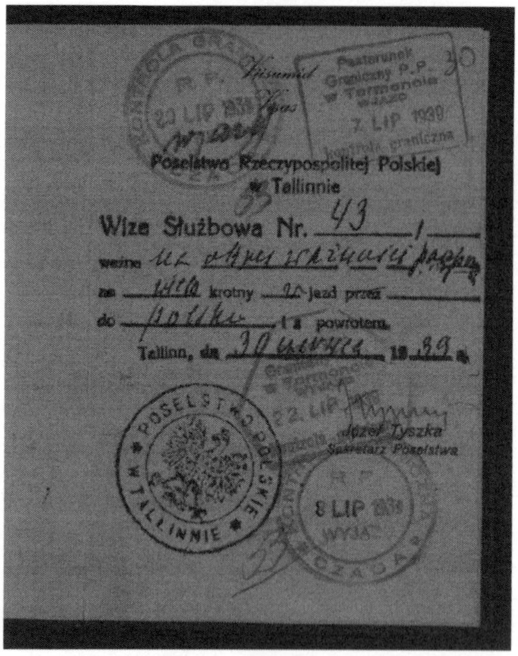

At Czaca, Artur Taska found my grandfather without difficulty and greeted him with a handshake. In his mid-twenties, the journalist had slicked-back dark hair and dark determined eyes behind horn rims. He edited the Valga-based *Southern Estonia* newspaper and was familiar with chemico-agricultural issues in the region. With their shared interest in chemistry, he and my grandfather quickly became friends. Artur Taska's brief was to cover the Budapest conference for the Estonian press, which he did under the byline 'A.T' or sometimes '-ska' (Taska abbreviated). The only other passengers with him and my grandfather in the compartment at this point were a Hungarian woman and her teenage daughter. The daughter wore a 'pin-up' hairstyle, Taska noted, with coloured ribbon bows and a 'modern-looking' dress patterned with Hungarian national motifs (eagles, crowns, double crosses). The mother, in her early thirties, had carefully manicured hands with 'deep red nails'. They both spoke German: most middle-class Hungarians spoke German.

Sunlight flooded the carriage as Polish officials boarded and checked visas. Rubber-stamped in my grandfather's passport (above the rubric: 'Business Visa No 43') was a Polish crowned eagle; his papers were in order. The Polish patrolmen put a circular blue CZACA stamp in all four passports before the train inched forwards out of Poland across the frontier into Nazi Slovakia. Everything was quiet at Čadca, as the station was now called. In this wolf-harbouring part of the Carpathian Mountains with its hazel spinneys and flower-filled summer meadows, the Slovak people lived under Hitler's shadow. Everyone in Slovakia – even Jews – had a swastika in their passports. Following the Nazi assault on Prague and the dismemberment of Czechoslovakia, in March 1939 Slovakia had seceded and allied itself gratefully to Hitler. By virtue of its position at the heart of Europe, Slovakia was integral to the Thousand Year Reich and was poised to become the gateway of the new Nazi empire into the Balkans and the occupied East. Swastika bunting fluttered along the station platform amid red, blue and white rosettes – the Slovak colours.

Frontiers have a dynamism all their own and can set off a reflex of unease. My grandfather, agitated, smoked cigarettes in the train corridor while the engine idled. An hour went by; two hours. Hens strutted over the rails. On the platform a boy was selling poppy seed cakes. The only sound, apart from the hissing of the engine, was the boy's voice, wheedling, insistent: cakes, hot cakes. More time passed. At last Slovak customs police with their red shoulder boards and peaked caps opened the carriage door with a 'Heil Hitler!' Did the four passengers give the Nazi salute in return? (One of the first decisions any foreign traveller had to make in Axis Europe in 1939 was whether or not to outstretch the arm in fascist greeting.) In Slovakia in what was once the Czech Republic the casual traveller might not see overt signs of Nazi oppression but the constant heiling and heel-clicking of railway and border staff told its own story. Hitler's march into Prague – tearing up the Munich Agreement as he went – legitimised Jew-hatred. Anti-Jewish demonstrations had erupted in the Slovakian capital of Bratislava – the old ugly story of broken windows and shouted insults – and Jews had been removed from the Slovak economy and subjected to expropriations. The new republic's sizeable German-speaking minority – about 150,000 in a population of 2 million – championed the solid burgherly values of *Kinder, Küche, Kirche* (children, kitchen, church). The notion of equality between the sexes, like the existence of homosexuality or avant-garde music, was dismissed by these Carpathian Germans as 'Jewish' and decadent. Many Poles thought the same way; after Germany, Poland was the first country to recognise Slovakia's existence.

The Slovak border police returned the Estonian passports to Taska and my grandfather with 'the compliments of the Führer', but they ordered the Hungarian women to get down off the train. Why? Because they did not have the 'correct visas' to continue on through Slovakia. Unruffled and unconcerned the officials demanded payment 'Now!', spitting out the word as if it were a bad taste. Close to tears the women beseeched the officials to reconsider. After much haggling, an on-the-spot fine of 20 Hungarian *pengős* (about £80 today) was levied. The Hungarians had been over-fined, but then Hungary, unlike Estonia, was not reckoned to be a Slovak-friendly state: Slovakia had gone to war with Hungary in 1938 over possession of a railway line along the Slovak–Hungarian frontier and the thousands of Hungarians who lived within the Slovak frontiers were agitating now for autonomy. The police put the money in their wallets and moved on to the next carriage. My grandfather tried to reassure the Hungarian mother and her daughter that customs inspectors everywhere in the world had the same rapacious hands. 'One day you'll be dining out on the episode over a nice glass of wine!', he said. The women smiled wanly and then, very bizarrely, expressed a surprise that Erich and Taska were Baltic nationals: they had assumed they were Japanese. Japanese? The 'awkward misunderstanding', as Taska called it, might have been prompted by the fact that Taska had a bespectacled studious air and Finno-Ugric upward tilting eyes that conceivably suggested those of Emperor Hirohito. (But this is dangerous territory – race scientists' territory.) The Hungarians mumbled an apology before the conversation moved on.

In the morning sun the train's shadow stumbled over fields and meadows. Carpathian villages glimpsed from the train were often no more than a cluster of farm buildings and roadside crucifixes watched over by a carved wooden church. Everywhere, Slovak folk were bent over their fields, carting the hay and leading their oxen. In this newly Germanised territory the swastika flamed a bright red. Presently a new name impinged: Banská Bystrica, a city in the Low Tatras, whose Gothic merchants' houses and medieval barbicans reminded Taska (he said) of the Hansa houses of Tallinn. Forward of the dining car a group of Finnish farm experts, rhythmically swaying with the train, were in high spirits in the glow of after-breakfast. At Zvolen, the final stop in the Slovak Central Mountains, a Slovak army officer got on. Enmeshed in pipe smoke on the platform was a huddle of dark-complexioned villagers in conical fleece hats and sheepskin jerkins. Romani lived in Slovakia in great numbers. Their Indo-Aryan language owed nothing to the adjacent Slav tongues and a great deal to Sanskrit. Hitler would deal with them.

The last of the morning sun came out as the train pulled into Lovinobaňa. From the carriage window Taska sneaked a photograph of an elderly Slovak man standing by the station bench with a boy – perhaps his grandson. The man has on a Tyrolean style felt hat. Visible on the wall above him is an enamel sign bearing the two-barred Slovak cross of the First Slovak Republic. After an hour the train approached the Hungarian border station of Losonc (today Lučenec in southern Slovakia), where passengers had to disembark and queue up outside an office with the sinister name 'National Centre for the Surveillance of Foreigners'. Hungary was still nominally a monarchy; a Royal Hungarian policeman looked through passports and paperwork with slow deliberation, darting occasional steely looks, before stamping them with *M.KIR* – 'Kingdom of Hungary'. For a fee of 50 fillérs (the 'penny' of interwar Hungary) my grandfather was granted a Hungarian visa 'posteriorly' as he had neglected to secure one back home in Tallinn.

Photo by Artur Taska, *Postimees*

As the wheels thudded along the tracks towards Budapest the Danube flowed alongside, less a waterway than a mirror reflecting vanished Austro-Habsburg lands. Lografts with Slovakian forest lumber drifted by. In its east-west meander from Bavaria to the Black Sea the Danube had united under the double-headed eagle Turkish Tartars, Russians, Ukrainians, Serbs, Bulgarian Muslims, Romani, Jews and Russian Old Believers: East to West. Few wished for the Habsburg Empire's return yet Hitler and Stalin between them were about to unleash a viciousness far greater than anything the German-Hungarian rulers in their Vienna fastness could have dreamed of. Jewish, Slav and Romani communities would disappear overnight as monarchical semi-tolerance was replaced by totalitarian intolerance. Fascism had become Europe's new 'sacred religion', observed Eric Ambler, whose espionage thrillers from this time (*Uncommon Danger, Epitaph for a Spy, Cause for Alarm*) anatomized the heart of Europe's darkness on the eve of war. Something new was beginning in the Danubian heartlands; quite what, no one yet knew.

After Szob the couplings strained and the train at last pulled in to Budapest-Keleti. The station, all elaborate gilt and stucco with marble Germanic Habsburg nymphs and satyrs under the architraves, had no equivalent in the Baltic. Over the platform hung a scent of charcoal smoke and fried paprika pods: unfamiliar Magyar smells. People hurried down the platform anxious to secure seats for Istanbul and other East-West connections. With Taska my grandfather shared a taxi for Pest on the Danube's left bank where they unpacked in the Danube Palace Hotel. Their rooms looked out across the Buda Hill and the needle spire of St Stephen's Basilica. The Hungarian capital – Evelyn Waugh wrote in 1938 for the *Catholic Herald* – 'forms one of the most beautiful cityscapes that exists along a river', adding: 'It is the most beautiful in Europe'.

Next day, Erich took in the German Jugendstil buildings with their green-tiled turrets and the window boxfuls of petunias. After Tallinn everything looked gigantic to him. Budapest had six hundred cafés. The Great Synagogue on Dohány Street – part Moorish, part Byzantine – was the largest synagogue in Europe and could seat 3,000 worshippers. Budapest was the banking centre of Central and Eastern Europe and the city's slick Austro-Habsburg haste and efficiency impressed Erich greatly. In the chandeliered Habsburg glory that was the Café Gerbeaud in Vörösmarty Square he ordered a breakfast of black tea with lemon, rose-leaf jam, croissants and chocolate buttercream sponge cake. Lunch consisted of pork and sauerkraut pungently flavoured with caraway. Except for the paprika, the Germanic fare was not so unlike Estonia's. The Ottomans had introduced the scarlet 'Turkish pepper' paprikia to Middle Europe in the sixteenth century and now it was ubiquitous. Erich sampled the Danube's coveted beluga sturgeon whose head tapered into a prehistoric-looking snout, as well as Lake Balaton pike-perch, which reminded him of the pike-perch of Estonia's Lake Peipsi. Lugubrious Bela Lugosi-like waiters brought him foaming steins of beer and shots of apricot vodka, sales of which had increased after the Duke of Windsor (the abdicated Edward VIII) was overheard to say he liked it during a visit to Budapest in 1937 as a guest of the dictator Horthy.

The conference delegates made their way to the Royal Palace for a reception. In his suit and tie Erich climbed up the hill to the Hofburg-like eminence that overlooked the Danube from Buda on the west bank. In the building's ornate Buffet Gallery with its marble statuary and suits of armour, the Hungarian Minister of Agriculture, Nicholas de Kállay, was busy introducing himself with a word of thanks and a handshake to the attendees. At one end of the gallery a string quartet played Strauss and at the other, flanked by sabre-carrying cavalrymen, stood His Serene Highness Admiral Horthy, the pro-German Regent of Hungary. Conservative and authoritarian, Horthy governed Hungary with all the prerogatives of a Habsburg monarch. He had introduced antisemitic legislations a decade before the Nazis; the latest of his anti-Jewish laws – promulgated in May 1939 – banned Jews from entering the legal profession and from owning property. To Horthy the Hungarian nation – the *natio Hungarica* – was a Christian bulwark against the threat of Red atheism and Jewry. It had been so against the 'civilizational threat' posed by Turks and Islam centuries earlier. Horthy's was a counter-revolutionary ethnic nationalist ideology that championed illiberalism over the parliamentary values of the West, and yet, like President Konstantin Päts of Estonia, he was not quite the dictator he was often labelled, being disliked by both the far Left and the far Right. Just as Päts had banned the neo-fascist VAPS movement in Estonia, Horthy had banned the Hungarian Nazi-fascist Arrow Cross Party (not least for its perceived threat to his own power). The press was freer in Hungary under Horthy than in Hitler's Germany, or, for that matter, in the Soviet Union or fascist Italy. People could talk freely on the streets of Budapest as they could not in Nazi Berlin. The problem for Hungarist populists and Hungarist patriots was – ironically – Hitler. On the other side of the Danube only a few miles from Budapest were blocks of ethnic, pro-Arrow Cross German *volk* who wished to be part of a united German race. The fear was that their restiveness might overflow into Hungary – and then what? In private Horthy little admired Hitler but he was far more virulently anti-Russian. To the north, across the Carpathians, one great nation was conspicuously absent from the congress delegates: Soviet Russia. Earlier in 1939 Horthy had joined Germany, Italy and Japan in the Anti-Comintern Pact against Moscow and he was no friend of International Communism.

Large and bulbous-nosed, in a black tailcoat and high stiff collar, Horthy exchanged polite, starchy talk with the delegates. He was a gifted linguist, with fluent French, Italian, Czech and Croatian and good English (James Joyce having been his English tutor in Austrian-Adriatic Trieste). As Estonia's official representative, my grandfather was required to shake hands with Horthy but what he made of the Magyar autocrat is not recorded. Perhaps they spoke of Hungarian–Estonian affinities and historic friendships. (The Magyars, like the Estonians, are reckoned to be a Finno-Ugric people: the roots of the Magyar language are Finno-Ugric.)** Erich had read in Estonian translation Ferenc Molnár's popular 1906 Hungarian novel *The Paul Street Boys,* about warring adolescents in turn-of-the-century Budapest, and maybe he mentioned that to Horthy. Or maybe not.

Later that evening, in the Westminsterian neo-Gothic Parliament building on the other side of the Danube, Hungarian captains of industry and banking lavished the delegates with champagne and platters of Danube sturgeon roe. My grandfather braced himself for the following day's round of conferences. These were held in the University of Technology and Economics. There, Erich gave a series of talks on dairy biochemistry and food preservation, which were 'well received' by fellow delegates (Taska reported in the Estonian newspaper *Päevaleht.*) In addition, he attended lectures on baking, distilling and wine-making, and sampled ersatz Hungarian foodstuffs made from dried banana powder. A Hungarian rice substitute based on husked wheat was found to be 'particularly tasty' (Erich reckoned) when cooked on charcoal-fired griddles. Hungary, self-sufficient in grains, could feed much of Central Europe with its rice substitutes. Displayed on stands and stalls in the university halls were samples of Hungarian chocolate pancakes and honeycomb confections. As a chain smoker my grandfather was drawn to the displays of Hungar-

** My grandfather was a member of Tartu University's 'Fenno-Ugria' cultural club, which fostered the study of Ural-Altaic customs and peoples, and which published the cultural magazine *Eesti Hõim* (The Estonian Tribe). Finno-Ugric Tribal Day, held each October in Estonia until it was banned by the Soviets in 1940, was an occasion for Finns, Karelians, Estonians, Hungarians and other Ural-Altaic folk to come together. It is today again.

ian tobacco leaves. He was intrigued by the Hungarian-patented 'Farinograph' apparatus that could measure in a matter of minutes the consistency and nutritional value of wheat flour dough; every Estonian bakery ought to invest in a 'Farinograph', he told Taska.

In a coach convoy the next morning the delegates were driven across the great Hungarian Plain – the *puszta* – beyond Budapest. A bitter-sweet smell rose from the maize fields which shimmered in the July heat. Budapest's rural belt with its plough horses and grazing moors was steppe-like in its vastness – the vastness of the central European hinterland. Over the hazy distance the sun was like a golden shield. Through the coach window Taska took photographs of the great plain as it rolled on flat as a ruler. Later that day the delegates were taken by steamer up the Danube to visit wine cellars and sample Tokay and other local whites. In Budapest's castle-like Agricultural Museum my grandfather wandered in a daze through halls dedicated to bee-keeping.

He could not understand why, in a country of such bountiful grain-growing, so many people starved. Children begged for food outside Budapest's bright-lit cafés and slept rough under the arches of Elizabeth Bridge. The aversion shown to the poor by the wealthy in Budapest was not lost on my grandfather. Old Austrian-Habsburg ideas concerning power and rank persisted; life was more caste-conscious and hierarchical in Budapest even than in Vienna. In the *puszta,* many of the big manorial estates were still in the hands of German-speaking foreign families who had supported the political interests of Austria and its Habsburg rulers. At the Budapest opera (where he went to see the Estonian prima donna Milvi Laid perform) Erich was amused by the sight of white-gloved attendants walking behind smokers with ashtrays at the ready. ('If you're a gentleman in Hungary you don't even have to carry your own cigarette case', he later told my mother axiomatically.)

Erich swam in the famous Gellért thermal baths near the Franz Josef Bridge where for the first time he became aware of Budapest's huge non-Magyar population – the so-called 'nationalities', the Serbs, Croats, Romanians and Slovaks who made up half of Hungary's total population. Budapest on the eve of the Second World War was a post-imperial city haunted by the collapse of the Habsburg, Ottoman and Tsarist empires and by the populations displaced by the First World War from Odessa, Kyiv, Smyrna and Istanbul.

On Margaret Island – Budapest's Coney Island – Taska and my grandfather went to see the 'Gypsy Violin King' Imre Magyari in concert. In his tuxedo, the enormously fat Magyari was outwardly a prosperous bourgeois Hungarian who played his soulful Tzigane music to adoring wealthy crowds. Taska (who may or may not have been pro-Nazi) was careful in his Estonian journalism to distinguish Magyari from the 'dirty, shabby' Romani 'wanderers' who 'infested' the foothills of Slovakia (and 'unfortunately' parts of Estonia too). With Erich he went to see Romani bands play on violins, piano-keyed accordions and the xylophonic hybrid peculiar to Hungary: the cimbalom. Folk rhapsodies after Liszt and Brahms rang out from the bars and hotels.

*

On 12 July while my grandfather was in Budapest, a German naval frigate anchored in Tallinn Bay. The *Admiral Hipper* and her German crew were received with full pomp by the Estonian government, but brawls broke out between the German sailors and Tallinners. Nazi Germany blamed the unrest on 'Communist provocateurs', but an Englishman in Tallinn at the time, Arthur Duncan-Jones, thought otherwise. Duncan-Jones reckoned the German naval visit had served to expose the gulf between Estonia's predominantly anti-German population and Estonia's increasingly pro-German government. Duncan-Jones happened to be the Dean of Chichester (and the grandfather of the late Shakespeare scholar Katherine Duncan-Jones); he was on a mission in Tallinn to report to the Church of England the attitude of the Baltic States towards Britain and Britain's waning sea power in the Baltic. The German war ship's presence in Estonian waters only aggravated Estonian fears of the German master–slave 'mentality' and German territorial 'ambitions' in the Baltic generally, said the Dean; there was, too, the Estonians' 'latent fear' of Russia, which had become accentuated that summer after Britain and France proposed the idea of a three-nation alliance with the Soviet Union against Nazi Germany. An obscure English aristocrat by the improbable hyphenated name of Admiral Sir Reginald Aylmer Ranfurly Plunkett-Ernle-Erle-Drax was dispatched to Moscow to open talks. The mode of his transport – he arrived by old cargo vessel – and his very name confirmed Soviet doubts about the mission's seriousness. (To his Soviet hosts the admiral boasted, in that nice polite English way, that he was a Knight of the Order of the Bath, which the Russian interpreter translated as the Order of the Bathtub.) Though the talks came to nothing, the British Consulate-Legation in Tallinn was unable to reassure the Päts administration that the alliance (should it be cemented) posed no harm to Estonia. The Estonian fear was of Red Army soldiers advancing with a rifle in one hand and Communist propaganda leaflets in the other. The pro-Päts Estonian newspaper *Uus Eesti* (New Estonia) launched a bitter attack on the Allies for their perceived attempts to accommodate Stalin. 'We have some experience of the Red Army – you in Britain appear to have forgotten this.' France was lambasted in no less sarcastic tones:

> And you, gentlemen in Paris, are you joking when you state in *Le Petit Parisien* (apparently in all seriousness) that if a pro-German uprising broke out in Tallinn or Riga, Moscow would interpret this as anti-Russian aggression, and take all steps necessary to protect its borders? If that is a joke, we think you are carrying it a little too far. Perhaps *Le Petit Parisien* could reveal to us the secret of who exactly in Tallinn or Riga is going to organise such a 'pro-German' uprising?

The truth is, Stalin had little interest in what he suspected would be a useless alliance with France and Britain (certainly it was not a pin's-worth of advantage to him to have an anti-Bolshevik British Conservative Order of the Bath admiral on his side.) Rather than enter into an Allied alliance against Hitler, Stalin preferred to make an alliance *with* Hitler. Behind closed doors he began to consider the unthinkable. By the summer of 1939, despite having built his political life on a hatred of the capitalist right, Stalin set his mind to what the Nazis might have to offer. Stalin did not know the meaning of scruple. His chief propagandist, Andrei Zhdanov, had stated in *Pravda* on 29 June that Britain and France did not actually want a military alliance with the Soviet Union, the implication being that Germany might wish for one instead. *Izvestiya,* another Kremlin mouthpiece, went so far as to speak of partitioning Poland between the Soviet Union and Germany. These were the first public hints from Moscow of Joseph Stalin's likely devil's pact with Adolf Hitler. In a move calculated to appease the Führer, Stalin started to cleanse the Soviet Foreign Ministry of Jews, replacing the veteran Soviet diplomat Maxim Litvinov (whose brother was a rabbi) with Vyacheslav Molotov as Commissar for External Affairs. Litvinov's Jewishness had long been a thorn in Stalin's side; anti-Nazi and pro-Western, Litvinov had been a signatory at the 1920 Tartu Peace Treaty between Estonia and Russia, but prolonged peace with Estonia was not what interested Stalin at this moment. Molotov had played a eager role in uprooting Trotskyists, *kulaki* and other 'vermin' from pre-war Soviet Russia, and was ready to wade through any depth of bloodshed to further his career. By appointing Molotov to External Affairs, Stalin opened a path to negotiations with Hitler, and Hitler understood well enough. His propaganda supremo Joseph Goebbels issued instructions to German journalists to desist from making 'sharp attacks on the Soviet Union until further notice'. Stalin, the embodiment of morbid mistrust, had placed his trust in Hitler.

*

Europe was about to detonate. But if anyone, looking in a crystal ball, had said that in less than a year not only France but all three Baltic States would fall to the dictators, no one would have believed them. On 14 July, while my grandfather was lecturing in Hungary, an Estonian schoolgirl called Nora Lossman arrived in Paris in time for the 150th anniversary celebrations of Bastille Day. A Tallinn army officer's daughter, Nora danced until dawn, drank champagne on the Champs-Élysées and watched the French military parades go by. On the rail journey home to Tallinn she witnessed what she later described as 'a placid acceptance of wholesale tyranny', which put a dark sobering shadow over the euphoric scenes she had witnessed in Paris. From the train window she caught a glimpse of Death's Heads and Brown Shirts on the march. Amid ear-splitting 'Heils' she watched Hitler Youth salute and ritualistically kiss a Nazi flag on a station platform, the flag badged (she thought) in the blood of a fallen comrade. The irony was that Nora's Estonian family counted many Baltic Germans as their friends. ('Some of them were more Estonian than the Estonians – good people', Nora recalled.) Her Polish mother, Maria Novicka, went horse riding with Baltic Germans in Tallinn's Kadriorg Park. The family's affection for German culture and the German language was so deep-rooted that it had not only survived the Estonian War of Independence but was apparently impervious to the Nazi Party's infiltration of the Baltic German ranks.

*

On his last day in Budapest my grandfather exchanged 30 Estonian kroon (£140 today) in a bank on Baross Square and with the Hungarian currency he bought a Magyar folk doll for each of his two daughters, and for his wife a hand-embroidered Magyar blouse. His chemist's budget stretched to a bottle of Hungarian 'Bull's Blood' wine, *Egri Bikavér*, known locally as the 'Vampire label' for its associations with Dracula's staked heart. (Erich noted with a philologist's curiosity that the Hungarian and Estonian words for 'blood' were cognate: *vér, veri.*) He packed the gifts in his suitcase and left the Danube Palace Hotel for the conference's gala closing ceremony in the Palatine Joseph University. The event, attended by the ever-watchful Admiral Horthy, was the talk of the Budapest gossip columns and society pages. Unsurprisingly Erich left Budapest with a feeling of regret. For ten days he had mixed with an international set of chemists, food scientists, oilseed plantation experts and plant pathologists; he had eaten a lot of rich Hungarian food, sat and smoked Sobranie cigarettes with Budapestian sophisticates and listened to Romani jazz. He marvelled at how the opportunity to travel through Poland, Slovakia and Hungary had fallen to a Tallinn chemist.

On the homeward journey to Estonia he shared a couchette with the White Russian chemist (and fellow Tartu University graduate) Konstantin Arensburger-Ivanov, who was known to be pro-German.*** The news from Moscow of a possible Allied pact with Stalin seems to have roused some vague uneasiness in Erich, as he went to some pains not to talk about it to Taska. On 21 July, a Friday, just as his train crossed the Slovak frontier into Poland, Wilfred Gallienne, the British consul in Tallinn, found himself cruising in a motor-boat on Lake Peipsi with the Estonian Foreign Minister Kaarel Selter. Soviet sentries on the Russian side of the lake watched them through binoculars. All appeared to be quiet. Lake Peipsi must be the 'quietest spot' in all the Baltic, Selter commented to Gallienne. 'Yes', Gallienne replied, 'a cure for jitters' – a reference to the generalised fear of war. The Russian frontier guards, who in the past had been so hostile and belligerent to their Estonian counterparts, now lavished them daily with gifts of chocolate and fruit. Selter was unable to deduce Russian intentions but he might have guessed that the Estonian border police were being 'sweetened' before Stalin opened negotiations with Hitler over the fate of Poland and the Baltic. Having fought against both the Germans and the Russian Bolsheviks in the Estonian War of Independence, Selter knew what to expect from a military occupation by either. As a sop to Gallienne he praised Neville

*** Among the Hungarians on the train were the much-loved Romani violinist-bandleader Jenő Farkas and the footballer László Keszei, who had played for Hungary at the 1936 Berlin Olympics.

Chamberlain, Britain's all-too trusting Prime Minister, as the 'finest gentleman in Europe'.

*

My grandfather came back to Tallinn with his passport covered in central-European visas. Elfriede was 'relieved to see him alive', my mother recalled. No harm had been done to her husband, and marital harmony was restored. Estonian journalists queued up to ask Erich for his impressions of Budapest but the only word he could think of was 'excellent': how to describe the sunset over the Hungarian Plain or the Romani music? He was more forthcoming on the subject of Estonian–Hungarian trade relations. 'Trade is unlikely to revive in the near future', he said, and he explained why: Estonia used to export 'vast quantities' of wood pulp cellulose to Hungary, but now that Hungary had acquired 'great forested regions' from the carcass of Czechoslovakia, 'Hungary could make all the cellulose it wanted from its *own* wood pulp'. Admiral Horthy was, though, interested in exporting paprika, which is 'rich in vitamin C and cheaper and better for us than pepper', my grandfather offered. As a parting shot he mentioned the pro-Hitler Duke of Windsor's fondness for Hungarian apricot vodka: perhaps Estonia could import some of that?

He reported his Hungarian findings to his boss Kaarel Liidak at the Ministry of Agriculture at 39 Lai Street in Tallinn, then took his family with him on holiday to Tartu close to the Soviet Russian border. The European, or 'world', war was now only weeks away. Tartu with its medieval ramparts and quaint cobbled streets seemed so far removed from the tide of world events as to be almost unreal. The hotels were full of tourists, there was a fever of entertaining and drinking in the nightclubs. Hitler was at Poland's gate, and darkness was about to fall on the unhappy continent of Europe.

Sequence

MARILYN HACKER

Charcoal sky, Thursday, a whole day of rain.
The vineyards, and the peach and apricot orchards need it, but I
sit upstairs here, not writing or reading, feeling an oblique
pain in my shoulders, my soul, descend again – the things I
didn't do, that it's too late to start, an essay, letters, I never wrote.
Tomorrow afternoon, I take the train back to the city, where I
lived, and don't want to live, though it was like desire for a
lover, a soul ache like ambition for years. The most contentious
conversation is with a friend, in writing, worse, on a phone or
with myself. Breathe out. A pause. Inspire.

*

Breathe out. A pause. Breathe in. Expire. Inspire.
An afternoon above weekend manifs.
Routine damp. Exhilaration. Grief, concentration. What comes
next? The fire of noon, or rain at midnight? The taut wire
messages crackle in, bringing their brief enigmas, queries,
responses. An opening leaf in sunlight. I'm lazy. I'm a liar
because my truth would be exhaustion, longing for elsewhere, for
a now long-vanished Thou, a life in its once plausible long morning.
I liked the walk to the épicerie, the baker, butcher, easy hours of Now.
Coffee, a croissant, possibility.

*

Coffee, a croissant. Possibility of morning, possibility of
heat and stasis: no rain, bad back, leaden feet.
Sans famille, sans patrie, presque sans abri, neither an exile nor a refugee.
One street doesn't mean more than the next street.
I like the bookshop, but no known-named merchant's greeting
starts my day: grocer, boulangerie, on my old street, or months in Montpeyroux.
'Ya ukhti', maybe, but not family.
Nobody asks 'What are you going through?'
or plans some trivial delight with me.
If I died in a hotel room, who would care ?
My daily limitations are – what's there.

*

My daily limitations are – what's there:
the underwear I wash out in the sink;
the morning coffee I decide to drink
in the hotel bar, café across the square;
three linen shirts I alternate, to wear
with two cotton-stretch pairs of jeans. I think
of my armoire, abandoned: green, black, hot pink
shirts, favourite shoes, a spare
everything in another colour if I like
it, Indian silk scarves, more shoes.
Too much of everything, little to lose
(if no one knocks me backwards on a bike).
And irreplaceable dictionaries,
when alphabets were my necessities.

*

Thirsts that were slaked in bars, but so much hunger
unassuaged. Even then, absences
accumulated, his, and hers, and his.
One could speak of longing, but not of anger....
Or of a glass jar filled with candied ginger
when home was home, a meeting-place of cities
in 400 square feet. I carry my keys,
still. What doesn't kill you makes you stronger?
What I can remember braces my spine:
a line of verse, prose, even a conjugation
in one of three, maybe four languages,
or, for the rest (bless translators) in translation.
The imperfect subjunctive, or John Donne
Ibn Arabi, Sappho, Maimonides.

*

When alphabets were my necessities,
a dictionary was a good companion
long afternoons when I was less alone
looking up: elbow; jackal; stroll; spring breeze,
laptop alight, real notebook on my knees,
Larousse Arabic–French laid open on
its stand, near my writing hand. Definition
opened a fan of possibilities.
Heatwave. I need a different kind of fan,
I need a different kind of concentration.
I search for, find them on line, The Temptations
singing, decades ago, 'I Wish It Would Rain',
that I once sang along to, that much younger,
in a bar, thirst slaked, but so much hunger.

*

Anne Donne, undone after twelve pregnancies...
'Les Droits de la femme et de la citoyenne...':
Olympe de Gouges hauled to the guillotine
for writing it, by revolutionaries.
Women could vote, with third grade literacy
in 1926, in Lebanon.
France, 1944.
                    Become a nun
to read? Shelter in libraries?
How many libraries consigned to flames?
How many Sapphos never learned to write ?
Literate anger doesn't know their names.
Illiterate, anger sets names alight.
I wrote this once, am writing it again
under a brutal sun, waiting for rain.

Baby Earth Environmentalism

ISABEL GALLEYMORE

By purchasing a pair of socks recommended for the purpose, I saved this Earth on Tuesday. Today, stopping by at my former school for their Earth Day fête, I'm at it again. Helping to fund an insect hotel in the school's playground, I hand over £1.50 for a planet Earth cupcake. Squidgily rendered in vanilla buttercream, its continents and oceans threaten to melt on this unusually warm spring day. For the first time this year, I've left the house without my coat. A few seagulls circle above. Strolling between the stalls set out in the car park and feeling mildly confused as to why every day isn't an Earth Day, I messily eat the planet.

This annual celebration of Earth that raises awareness of the need to protect the environment began on 22 April 1970, just a few years after the planet was first photographed from space. In the recorded conversation between members of the Apollo 8 crew, there's clear excitement at the prospect of capturing the world through the camera lens. Taking part in this unscheduled activity, the astronaut William Anders pressed the shutter lens and produced 'Earthrise': our planet half hidden by the shadow of the moon. Some said that the Earth was playing peek-a-boo. Later, a more formal portrait was taken by astronauts on Apollo 17, a picture that became widely known as 'The Blue Marble'.

Through these images, the unthinkable largeness of the planet had been reduced to something seemingly diminutive, dinky. As the comparison of Earth to a glass marble suggests, astronauts felt compelled to give language to this sudden shift in scale. 'It suddenly struck me', Neil Armstrong explained, 'that tiny pea, pretty and blue, was the Earth.' Trying to make sense of this new perspective, similar metaphors emerged: our planet was a 'tiny apple', a 'lonely speck', a Christmas 'bauble'. An entirely new perspective of ourselves and our home was gained. People were awe-struck; or should that be aww-struck?

*

A baby's face might seem to have exclusive rights to cuteness. Large eyes compete against chubby cheeks in taking up real estate on the face of my friend's two-month-old son. But cute is also the 'p' of puddle and pumpkin. It's the simplicity of a button. Wide-ranging and often weird, the voltage of cuteness is unpredictable and can be uncomfortable: it's my kitten's porn-pink toe beans, a mosquito stuffed toy, a lost mitten, the idea of a dejected mushroom. Cuteness likes vulnerability and so it often adheres to the teeny-tiny. Even that which weighs over six billion trillion tons – if seen from the right angle or baked until light and fluffy – might be thought enchanting or precious.

'I think the tenderness that lies in seeing the Earth as small... is probably one of the most valuable things we have now', claimed the anthropologist Margaret Mead in the presence of a crowd celebrating Earth Day for the first time in New York City; a crowd that would have been familiar with 'Earthrise' and 'The Blue Marble' images. As a baby's cute features are said to trigger an instinct to love and care in us, so observing the Earth as little and frail brought about a new desire to protect it. Prompted by seeing the Earth photographed in this new way, Earth Day was only one part of a larger international environmental movement that prioritised ecological and spiritual unity. On *Sesame Street*, girls and boys were filmed throwing and catching a blow-up globe as if this were the epitome of the coordinated teamwork we would need going forward. A couple of decades later, promoting his pop hit 'Heal the World', Michael Jackson held a little Earth to his chest.

*

Thinking I recognise one of my former teachers, I fold the grease-sogged cupcake paper into my pocket and busily involve myself in the table of raffle items. One of these is an Earth plushie. Possessing stunted arms and legs, this cuddly cosmic companion has a quizzical expression as if the Earth is surprised to have found itself inhabiting this form. Another item on the raffle table, which is garnering much excitement, is a dollhouse.

In *The Pillow Book*, completed in early 1002, the Japanese author Sei Shōnagon wrote a list which included 'dollhouse furniture and tableware, a tiny floating lotus leaf plucked from a pond. Little hollyhock flowers'. Where other translations have used the word *beautiful*, Joshua Paul Dale's recent interpretation reads: 'Indeed all small things, no matter what they are, all things are exceedingly *cute*'. The claim is worth testing. Bring to mind a few neutral or uncute things, then imagine each downsized: a mini bottle of paracetamol; a microscopic Yellow Pages; a tiny tombstone. The latter doesn't need to be imagined, it exists. Made by London Zoo, the tombstone – or should I say tombpebble – commemorates Turgi, a Polynesian tree snail and the last of the species *Partula turgida*. It was inscribed '1.5 million years BC to January 1996'.

The miniature, according to Susan Stewart, invites us 'into the infinite time of reverie'; a statement that goes some way in assuaging the guilt I feel at whimsically enjoying the Lilliputian tombstone in the midst of this sixth mass extinction. All things that are little appear to wriggle out of context and perhaps reality altogether. As Stewart says, 'once we attend to the miniature, the outside world stops, is lost to us'. What does this mean for the miniature earths that proliferate in current environmental rhetoric? Googling 'Save the Earth' prompts countless images of the planet cradled by pairs of hands: hands of suited business men; hands disembodied and anonymous; a woman's immaculately manicured hands, elderly hands bestowing the Earth into the patiently-cupped hands of the young. One could be presenting a gift to a sweetheart or lifting an injured duckling from harm. Instead, each and every example presents the vast planet we are living on.

Although seeing our planetary home from space is understood to have prompted a new and vital wave of environmentalism, our current fetish for little earths may well suggest the opposite. If the act of miniaturization gives way to playful daydream, there's a suggestion that we are escaping the terrifying truth of our frail existence on Earth with these well-meaning handfuls of planet and smiley-faced worlds.

*

Changing our perspective of Earth has changed our relationship to it. As the planet has moved in our imagination from being impossibly large to curiously and cutely 'smol'; as the planet has been harmed and irreversibly damaged by us, she no longer seems to fill the role of Mother Earth. The Earth of today is needy, demanding. The Earth of today wants to be mothered.

A ballpoint pen I bought last summer reads 'Save the World' along its side. Nested in the 'o' of 'world' is a baby-looking Earth with sleep-closed eyes and coy smile. In among the many Earth Day posters that pupils have made and pressed to the windows of the dining hall, one crayoned world sprouts a speech bubble from its downturned mouth: 'Save me'. Diddums, I think, scanning the posters again, half expecting to see a drawing of Earth in a nappy, a dummy plugged somewhere into the global north.

This shift in power seems baked into the phrases we use. Previous environmentalist eras talked of 'Managing' the planet or 'Battling' for Earth. 'Saving' may seem somewhat softer. After all, to save is to safeguard and to set free. Yet, the positioning of ourselves as saviours – and saviours of Earth at that – brings with it extraordinary hubris. Varaha who appears in the form of a boar, being the third avatar of the Hindu deity Vishnu, lifts the planet between his tusks and restores it to the universe. Referencing the Christian God in my eclectic school choirs each week, we'd sing the African-American spiritual 'He's got the whole world in his hands'. Thirty or so years later and feeling a little rusty with the lyrics, I look them up on my phone. The search results surprise me by almost exclusively replacing 'he' with 'we'. I feel sorry for the pupils who sing this version today. While the revision suggests greater inclusivity, it gestures towards fantasy and impossible responsibility.

*

In geography classrooms across the country, there's a high probability of finding a little globe, a modern and accessible version of those set on wrought-iron axes, encased in brass rings – a gentleman's plaything and a common prop in movie scenes in which kings and parliamentarians discuss empire building and geopolitical strategy. Whispers of our current god complex encircle such items and grow increasingly louder with the events that led to 'Earthrise' and 'The Blue Marble' photographs. If leaving the Earth's atmosphere and rocketing into the heavens isn't evidence enough of our divine ambitions, then the circumstances in which such missions were made must be. Apollo 8 and 17, from which the photographs were taken, were both significant assets in the space race that was driven, in no small part, by anxieties concerning Russian surveillance and the Cold War. Each in their own way implied not only a new human omniscience over Earth, but also the potential for humanity to wipe itself out along with all other biological life.

'A scientist has a test tube full of sheep', writes Russell Edson in one of his classically absurdist poems. At first, the scientist wonders benignly if 'he should try to shrink a pasture' for the tiny sheep. Then, 'if it is possible to shrink something out of existence'. A few lines later,

> He wonders if they could be used as a substitute
> for rice, a sort of woolly rice...
> He wonders if he shouldn't rub them into a red paste
> between his fingers.

Over the last few weeks, Instagram has saturated my feed with miniature livestock animals. A tiny 'teacup' pig one day, a micro-mini cow the next. The cow is called Mouse, wears a dog harness and sleeps indoors on a futon outfitted in polka dots. How we seesaw from violence to care and back in the teeniest, tiniest company.

In space, Armstrong recalled 'I put up my thumb and shut one eye, and my thumb blotted out the planet Earth'. But, unlike Edson's scientist who takes on a godlike role in creating and destroying life, Armstrong didn't think about the possibilities of pressing and obliterating the world. 'I didn't feel like a giant', he admitted, 'I felt very, very small.'

*

Nearing midnight and resisting the urge to sleep, I often find myself doom-scrolling on my phone. Inevitably I read a news item on our exceeding of climate change tipping points. When I finally turn off the light, I discover that the world is once again a pea. But not the pea that Armstrong described from the window of his spacecraft. This time, the Earth is the pea from the fairy tale. All night I am a princess sleeping fitfully because the world presses through all the many comforts I inhabit.

It's not just tipping points that provoke this unease. It's the ballpoint pen with baby face tucked into the o in 'world', which gave me two weeks of use before its ink gave up. The desirability of cute commodities is so powerful because it taps into a mothering instinct. I bought the pen because, to some extent, I wanted to take care of that baby world. Now, I'm left with the prospect of polluting the environment with this piece of plastic for the next thousand years. The aesthetic of cuteness demands care and love whilst simultaneously – and paradoxically – suggesting triviality and disposability. Made from polyester, the cuddly Earth plushie on the raffle table is no different. For one lucky winner, this is an Earth that is resilient; once tired of it you can throw it away, but it's going nowhere fast.

*

Motion sickness is caused by sensory confusion. I've experienced it in a friend's car, several ferries, train seats facing backwards and, in Disneyland Paris, a jerky mouse-shaped buggy. Apparently, I'm experiencing it again standing still and watching this current spectacle: the head teacher of this school is dressed in an inflatable Earth costume while handing out packets of wildflower seeds. I am observing the world fitted over his slim-hipped, six-foot figure and, at the same time, I'm inhabiting this world with its surface area of 510.1 million kilometres squared. My body, eye and inner ear send conflicting signals to my brain.

The scholar Timothy Clark would likely diagnose me with a chronic 'derangement of scale'. In his writing on the Anthropocene, Clark pauses on Bill Anders's description of Earth as a Christmas bauble, the way he saw it on his Apollo 8 mission. If we extend the metaphor, then something very peculiar happens: 'A family living room at Christmas, with its tree and decorations, becomes in a sense immediately "bigger" than the planet in the window of a space capsule, even as, simultaneously, that room and its Christmas tree ball have never been smaller.'

The image of the woman's immaculately manicured hands cupping the planet brings about a similar derangement, especially if you catch sight of her wedding ring. Which laws and conventions are being followed in this scenario – planetary or domestic? Is she married to... the world? And where exactly is she? If she holds the Earth, then presumably she must live somewhere beyond it.

*

Humming and hissing, the Earth produces sounds we cannot hear. Magnetic fields push through particles creating a 'chorus wave', so called because when converted to audio the waves sound like the dawn chorus. Having listened to a clip, I can't help but think the whistling sound is more suited to an otherworldly milkman. And then there are the other sounds that Earth can make. 'She walks around with the Earth in her mouth all day long', a dog-owner writes on behalf of her dog, who has recently been treated to an 'Earth Dog Toy'. Another reviewer notes helpfully 'they squeak (not obnoxiously)'.

In his study of 'auditory cuteness', musicologist David Huron assesses little bells, certain bird chirps and smaller animal calls. Ultimately, he identifies squeeze toys as delivering the cutest of cute sounds. These playthings have, in most cases, 20ml of volume, which approximately matches a human infant's vocal tract. The park near this former school of mine is prolific with man's best friend. Next time I'm passing, I tell myself, I'll keep my eyes and ears peeled for a baby's cry passing itself off as the Earth and gripped between the sharp teeth of a dog.

*

In our current environmental moment, the words 'Save the Earth' flock together like those kitschy ceramic ducks on a living room wall. And like the ducks, more often than not the phrase is issued mechanically; its original vitality many times removed. In an optimistic mood we might feel that when we talk about saving the Earth we are talking about saving rhinos and the climate, oceans from plastic and overfishing, saving dandelions, microbes, mosquitoes, soil. In other words, saving the world means saving *all* of it. Doesn't the baby Earth of our making deserve our unconditional love? With less hope and more cynicism, we might ask whether the idea of saving the Earth is for Earth's sake or merely our own. The cute anthropomorphized world that cries 'save me' is not the world at all. The voice is a human one; it is us asking us to save us.

How would the ash tree in my garden go about saving the Earth? And the blackbird nesting on its branch? The worm in its torch-bright beak? How to organize a multi-species consultation to learn from all these different perspectives when even a small change in our own perspective can throw us off? After Earth was 'saved' onto colour film by an astronaut on Apollo 17, but crucially before it was released to the public and became a catalyst for environmentalism, the image was manipulated to ensure the South Pole was at the 'south' and Africa the 'right' way up. It's possible to love the Earth when seen from 29,000 kilometres, but out of the question if the Earth were 'upside down'.

Calling out to her friend, a little girl rushes past me with hands cupping a blue marble. It turns out to be an item another child lost earlier in the playground. A small war kicks off as to who should keep it. Jostled, the little girl drops the marble, but doesn't immediately realise. Her hands still cupped but empty, she appears for an instant to be begging.

A mouse from my cat; the hummus snack pot from the landfill; a little bit of money, myself from the rain when I remember my umbrella. These are the things I know I can save.

Shadows have begun to appear at new angles. Tired and hungry, it's not just the children that begin to squabble, but the parents too. On this enormous carousel we call home, we're being gently turned away from the sun. Earth Day is coming to an end. Every last planet has been eaten. On the melamine table, a blue sticky smear of ocean.

Conversations with God

DARÍO JARAMILLO

translated by Richard Gwyn

1

The first time that God spoke to me, He was disguised as a snake.
It was hard to accept that someone like God should turn up in such
    a surprising form, but that's what He's like, always clever, clever
    like a snake, yes, exactly like a snake.
What's more, there's the precedent: the devil came to Eve disguised as
    a serpent. No one would expect God to use the same trick.
    That's exactly why He used it. It was the best kind of deception.
That day was just a sort of test. He told me He was God. I believed Him
    and in that consisted the proof, that I believed Him. If I had doubted Him,
    He would never have spoken to me again. But I believed Him.
He told me He was the Everlasting Father. That He had created the world
    and controlled almost everything. Almost. But He didn't clarify what things
    He doesn't control.
I think He didn't explain this to me for dramatic effect. He left me in suspense.
I am still in suspense.

2
I am still in suspense because the second time God spoke to me,
I didn't see Him. It was the crack of dawn. A Monday. He spoke
in my ear and asked me to take notes, that He was going to dictate.
He said: this is my third attempt at creation. I am perfect,
but my inventions are not. This time my invention was
of an intelligent being.
He said: intelligent, but greedy; intelligent, but avaricious;
intelligent, but filled with hate; intelligent but capable
of killing his fellow beings.
He said other things which one day I will tell you.
Yes, I know, I'm used to that reaction: of course you people are thinking
that I'm crazy. But I am not crazy. But you will insist that only
a crazy person says that God spoke to him.
What you don't know is that God warned me that you would call me crazy.
And He also said that He was not going to speak to those
sane people who are so crazy that they believe it's impossible that
God should speak to them.

7
Sometimes God gets metaphysical and I understand little of what
He tells me. He guesses that I understand little or nothing, and I hear Him laugh,
and then He yells at me: learn this phrase by heart:
The atheists are right. I don't exist. I am prior to existence. I am the word.
The word without an owner.
I am the word without existence that gives existence to the atheists.
Another day He said to me: the atheists know much more about me than I do.

9
I am growing in confidence. Last night God asked me: if you
were God, would you be happy?
Let me think about my answer, I suggested, and He, who is eternal,
reprimanded me:
Do not forget that I read your mind, miserable creature. If you are thinking
to mollify me, I will know.
I answered Him: then you do not have to ask me, because you already
know the reply.
It's not easy being God, he said speaking to Himself, with me as a mere
witness, everyone criticises the world but no one offers suggestions.
You complain, my God, you complain – and yet it is clear that nothing hurts you at all.
Then God went away and only came back to talk to me again much later.

10
He told me,
several times He told me
Don't try to understand time, don't go chasing what only drags
on and on, watching the clock prolongs the wait, as you know.
Forget about time, don't explain it because you will lie, don't understand it
because then you will go mad,
don't meddle with time – He warned me as if time were the forbidden tree of paradise –
I'm telling you for your own good: leave time alone, don't meddle with it, don't
meddle with it, He said again and again.
If at all possible do not wind your clock, better that you learn to guess the hour,
He told me and He smiled. I have never seen the smile of God, but it is easy
to tell when His words are accompanied by smiles.
All of this God told me: time is one of God's favourite topics.
One day I asked Him:
If you want me to forget about explaining time, why then
do you talk to me so much about time?
He answered me gravely: Time is the secret of the recipe, the ingredient
that nobody will ever know.

I was bold with this God absorbed in mystery:
You speak as if you yourself were wary of time.
Very great are the silences of God, and that day I felt the gravity of his silence.
Like an icy wind, His silence penetrated me.
At length God, who is not God for nothing, let out a malicious chuckle
and told me:
You know eternity from the outside. So, in the same way,
I know time, from outside of it.
Now I think this: God is patient because He does not wait. God
does not know waiting, He does not know anxiety, is ignorant
of evil and unaware of time.

21
Sometimes I have my doubts.
I don't know what to do with those who speak in my name.
I can't figure it out.
It's as if they robbed my name, as if an impostor signed with my name.
Only because I am God can I grasp the number of individuals who speak
in my name.
There are priests and shamans, healers and wise men, prophets and clergymen,
ministers and...
(I will have to consult the dictionary. There are times when a book knows more
than God. To say nothing of Google).
I'm speaking about those who speak in my name,
– pontiffs, vicars, *mamos*, shamans, sages –
not to mention those who think they are God.
They intone their words in the certainty that they are gods.
What am I going to do with them?
They slander me, they discredit me,
It's already complicated enough being God without some miserable creature
coming along and claiming they are God.
They make me look ridiculous, they distort me.
I don't know what I'm going to do with the poets.
I don't know what I'm going to do with the poets.
I don't know what to do with that air of expertise that they give off.
Their instrument is the word, their end is the word.
They are unaware that the word is me.
I don't know what I'm going to do with the poets who seem to be
in touch with all the mysteries
and speak about death as if they know it.
I don't know what I'm going to do with the poets,
so lucid, so enlightened, so initiated in all that is most profound.
Maybe – and mind you, God also has His doubts – maybe add them to the list of
false representatives of God,
popes, prophets, presbyters, provosts, preachers, pulpit-grabbers,
peripatetic priests without pardon, gluttons of the superfluous word,
narcissists of their verse, the poets are bad children,
that's why I made them vain and idle,
in God's name
– and I am God –
I don't know what to do with the poets.

23
God is perfect but on occasion he makes mistakes.
He told me this without my understanding him,
as I am always left without understanding:
Explain to me with an example – I dared to interrupt.
And then only subtle silence, doubtful silence, or irritated silence
because I interrupted him, or indifferent silence,
how difficult to interpret silence, I was thinking,
I was thinking that when He said:
My mistake was this species. And I, who know everything, was not
unaware that it would all turn out badly if I allowed your species to appear.
It was an error.
It was an error.
It was an error.
He said it three times and, without opening my mouth, I insisted to him that he clarify
himself to me and there was another silence and another on top of that and then
an ironic or sardonic laugh:
If you all weren't my mistake, you wouldn't be asking that question.
And as he moved away, he added:
Stupidity does more damage than depravity.

30
I'm sure you've heard this saying: no one is perfect.
He said that to me. It was the middle of the night and I was awake in the darkness.
The silence was so big that it gave shelter to all that could be heard.
Inside myself I was in silence, also.
No one could hear that silence.
And suddenly, He began to whisper to me and everything was sublime:
He was speaking and yet all was silent.
No one is perfect: I came up with that, God told me in a whisper,
I came up with that, one night when I discovered that I will never be able
to dance.
Without knowing it, humans improved my invention by making music.
He said that, and then said:
I am not perfect, I cannot dance.
But I make up for that by the pleasure of listening to a piano in the dead
of night, when I speak in the insomniac ear of a man
who will not return to sleep that night.

Eleven Poems

STEVE MALMUDE

Selected and introduced by Miles Champion

The poems that follow, together with the pamphlet *Lifeguard*, recently published by London small press Distance No Object, constitute Steve Malmude's first publications in the United Kingdom. A second-generation poet of the New York School, Malmude's name is too often left off that list, perhaps because his work is so differently distinct, or perhaps because he was too busy – or too literarily elsewhere – to join, or to be invited to join, the club. He has always made his poems slowly and carefully, rearranging and reworking his stanzas – usually quatrains – in a process he has likened to that of a teenager, comb in hand, endlessly experimenting with their hair in front of a mirror. His oeuvre is modest, but of the highest quality, and unlike anything else in American letters.

Stephen David Malmude was born in New York City on 4 January 1940, to parents of Ukrainian Jewish and German Lutheran extraction. His father, Simon Malmude (an Americanisation of Malamud, the Hebrew word for teacher), previously an actor in the Yiddish theatre on Second Avenue and the host of a radio programme in which he analysed people's handwriting, devoted the bulk of his life to a failed attempt to pass himself off as an advertising executive, on the back of an entirely fictitious CV. With no money coming in, Malmude's mother, Alice Probst, was forced to provide for the family, working as a nurse and, after receiving her doctorate from New York University, as a teacher. The family moved to Brooklyn in 1946 – urban planner Robert Moses was razing their neighbourhood in Lower Manhattan – and Malmude attended Brooklyn Tech, where he became enthusiastic about Shakespeare and poetry. Bohemia was a known quantity: Malmude's uncle, Joachim Probst, was a painter (primarily of religious themes) who frequented the same Greenwich Village bars as the Abstract Expressionists, and whose non-objective works – black ink washes on a white ground – had a decisive (if unacknowledged) influence on his close friend Franz Kline. When Malmude declared his intention to be a poet, his father, perhaps a little richly, recommended a backup plan, but, after a semester of studying engineering at Queens College, Malmude switched to English and classics, and fell in love with poetry. He was on the swimming and water polo teams, obtained his lifeguard certification and ran waterfront camps during the summers.

After graduating, Malmude joined the United Brotherhood of Carpenters and Joiners of America and worked as a carpenter in residential construction in the Bronx. He settled into a routine of working for six months of the year and spending the other six writing poetry and living the life that was to be had so cheaply on the Lower East Side. The earliest poem presented here, 'Danang', dates from this period. It is an astonishing poem by any measure, and quite staggering as an early effort by a young poet. Intended from the outset as an anti-war poem, it was initially conceived as an exchange of letters between a soldier in Vietnam and his girlfriend back home. Feeling that the poem was becoming unwieldy and unworkable, Malmude pulled out the parts he liked best and arranged them as a monologue. The poem's corkscrew form and light-footedly dense sound patterning owe much to Malmude's failed attempts to translate the poetry of François Villon such that its rhymes were upheld. He was reading Chaucer at the time, and aware that the rhymes and rhyme schemes he found so compelling were significantly easier to achieve in Middle English and French. Aside from a few college friends who had also moved to the Lower East Side, he was writing in isolation; he read *Poetry* magazine and the academic poets of the day, and admired Jules Laforgue, Robert Lowell's *Imitations* and the Pound of *Personae* (but not the *Cantos*). Testing his crampons on Black Mountain, he responded to Robert Creeley's dry New England brevity but found Charles Olson's conception of the poet's role off-putting.

Feeling that publication in the *New Yorker* would validate him as a poet – would allow him to call himself a poet – Malmude devoted considerable time and energy to having one of his first poems, 'The Goat Man', published there. Correspondence with the *New Yorker*'s poetry editor, Howard Moss, led to several in-person meetings, but 'The Goat Man' was ultimately dropped (Moss: 'It's just *not* a *New Yorker* poem.'). Malmude's partner at the time suggested he might fare better at the nascent Poetry Project at St. Mark's Church, a few blocks away. He attended one of the Monday night open readings hosted by Jim Carroll and read 'Danang' and 'The Goat Man', along with other exceptional poems. Carroll introduced him to Larry Fagin, whose storied Adventures in Poetry imprint issued Malmude's first book, *Catting*, in 1972. He became a regular at the Project, preferring to sit alone at readings but becoming friendly with Jim Brodey, Michael Brownstein and Lewis Warsh, among others, and, later, Rudy Burckhardt and Edwin Denby.

While looking for a union job in 1968, Malmude walked past a Jewish community centre under construction, the 14th Street Y, with an indoor pool. He decided to leave carpentry and work as a lifeguard, soon becoming the director of the aquatics programme at the Y, a job he held for ten years. His poem 'To Portland' dates from this time, and is a highly charged, almost hallucinatory catalogue of things seen, primarily while travelling back and forth between house and hospital during the birth of his first daughter, Anna: 'the gas / station settling on a lily... spider / webs across the menses of the mice... A squirt of pigeon stool / like the backbone of a herring... My / semen falling down in water / like a clown in pain.'

Accustomed to writing his poems longhand in a ruled notebook, Malmude learned to type after being given a typewriter by a Hungarian employer who dictated letters he wanted sent to the German government (he was seeking reparations, his family having been killed, and he enslaved, by the Nazis). His poems increasingly took the form of short-lined, blocky quatrains separated from each other by double line breaks, a form he adopted to make his poems visually recognisable, and because he liked the quatrains (and non-linearity) of classical Chinese poetry (indeed, he increasingly viewed his own quatrains as combination logogram-pictographs). Rhyme remained an essential ingredient: as much of it as possible, as concentratedly as possible. The four-quatrain poem is Malmude's version of a sonnet, and he regards another favourite poem length, the two-page poem comprising fourteen quatrains, as a variant sonnet form. Both poem lengths offer convenience: they are compositional matrices into which a great variety of subject matter can be instilled (or, one might say, collaged).

He began to write down anything he heard, read or thought that could be accommodated in a quatrain. These stanzas – which number in the thousands – are contained in two overflowing binders that he regards as his palette, and are arranged by ascending number of characters (letters and spaces). One of Malmude's early compositional methods was to arrange his quatrains in ascending character count, such that the resulting poem, after a wispy start, ends up decidedly buff from the workout. 'Paragon', the first poem made in this way (around 1975), begins:

You stay
black against night
and white
against day

behind drapes
four hours
on all fours
down fire escapes

that is, with quatrains of forty-seven and fifty-two characters. It ends:

your grandfather's
corduroy pants argued
like pinking shears
crossing the Williamsburg

God mixed up the builders' speech
in other words
he made some talk in one language
and some another

– quatrains of eighty-three and ninety-three characters. Arranging quatrains in ascending character count or rearranging – playing with – quatrains of a similar size have remained Malmude's principal compositional modes. He has never written in a linear fashion and will run a finished poem backwards if he thinks it will yield a more interesting result.

If this *is* collage, it is collage at its most humanised. When Malmude selects a quatrain from his palette to insert into a poem in progress, he frequently reworks it so substantially that the source quatrain is no longer discernible. His palette, then, is not only always being added to, but also endlessly generative. The use of collaged material, whether from Graham Greene or Howard Stern, and regardless of the degree to which it is combed and recombed, also addresses the issue of vocabulary: Malmude is attuned to the fact that the vocabulary of recognition far exceeds the vocabulary of use, particularly in everyday spoken American English.

When he returned to carpentry in 1978, Malmude's union membership had lapsed and he picked up small jobs where he could, often working with artists and sculptors, and learning from the city's migrant workers, especially Irish carpenters and West Indian stonemasons who had come to the United States from the UK. He took a civil service exam in 1987 and worked as a carpenter for the Housing Authority until his retirement in 2001, when he left the city and relocated to Limerick, Maine, where he has worn various hats – substitute teacher, volunteer firefighter, swimming instructor – and been involved in local politics.

The persona behind Malmude's poems is that of the New York working guy – specifically, the New York Jewish working guy. Occasionally a swagger, unmistakably male, outpaces aesthetic sensibility: one senses that the poet enjoys his charisma, thinks of himself as someone who can handle himself across a range of situations, from practicality (he has a trade, can build) to pugilism ('You talking to me?'), and that he is proud of his body, its athleticism and strength. Now a trim and genial grandfather at eighty-four, Malmude readily admits that, as a young man, he wasn't particularly pleasant. The St. Mark's peers he most quickly befriended were fellow New Yorkers, and one notes later poet friendships with other New York Jewish working guys, such as Ted Greenwald, whom Malmude met when Greenwald was throwing bundles of the *Village Voice* from the back of a truck. Nevertheless, Malmude's poetry leaves a taste (I hesitate to use the word *metallic*) that is entirely its own, and his craftsmanship is so fine that it is difficult to fully account for this. Part of it, certainly, is the ready recognisability of his calligraphic quatrains, and the arresting – sometimes shocking – vividness of their content. Part of it, too, is the wistful melancholy the reader feels as she acknowledges that the blue-collar worker who wears their erudition so lightly is increasingly an anachronism in our time. Indeed, this is a poetry so ripe with lived experience that the reader is forgiven for shedding a nostalgic tear. But, beyond the respiratory dovetailing of working life and writing – the way one creates a rhythm for the other – there is something else, a more nebulous quality that seems to undergird both the appearance and subject matter of the poems, and which might most plainly be stated as a vertiginous, but stoic, awareness of the rootlessness that is the condition of the non-native American.

Given that Malmude spent half of his early writing years on the Lower East Side, at a time when the community of poets around St. Mark's was coming into flower, it is surprising that he wasn't more frequently published – until, that is, one considers the careful seriousness of his work. Two further, modest books were published, *From Roses to Coal* in 1980 and *I Got to Know* in 1997 (the former containing seven of *Catting*'s eighteen poems), and a ninety-two-page selected poems, *The Bundle*, now out of print, in 2002. While Malmude is not without diffidence, the relative scarcity of his published work can be attributed to the fact that his ambitions have always been for his poems, not for any sort of poetry career. He writes – has always written – for the pleasure of doing so, and is perhaps unusually prone to the self-doubt and self-questioning that so often afflict poets of the first stripe (he was given a substantial boost when Creeley selected 'Perfect Front Door' for the *Best American Poetry* series in 2002). And so it is that he has been assigned the somewhat dubious sobriquet of *neglecterino* – a poet who, in Fagin's terms, has 'fallen through the cracks'. He keeps excellent company there, of course: Alan Fuchs, Samuel Greenberg, Emily Greenley, Thomas Hood, Richard Kolmar, Clere Parsons, David Schubert, John Thorpe and Rebecca Wright – to name only a few – spring quickly to mind. The twenty-first century has been good to neglecterinos so far: young editors have made the work of Mark Hyatt, Joan Murray and Alfred Starr Hamilton available to new audiences, and we also have the complete poems of Iliassa Sequin. It is entirely reasonable to hope – to expect – that Steve Malmude's singularly striking body of work will be next.

Danang

The system shouts
a phoneme.
Phraze-yard
touts
hazard
an acronym

for DMZ
but it's 'demise'
or 'dooms'.
Such whimsy
booms
our marihuana highs,

whoreson
mother-of-pearl
fetishes.
But Thorazine
re-etches
knurl

on the handles.
A troop shuffle
destroys
the mandalas
of our stories.
Bivouac oval

recurs:
new bases'
wriggling
loudspeakers'
rigging;
oasis

particulars;
the intercom
transmits the burbles
of the water coolers;
the portables
succumb

to interference,
mucking
an aural
clearance.
As for our morale,
it's bucking

peace offers
which cloy
women's pity.
A soldier suffers
every city
but Hanoi,

resigned
to that outré
sort of tact
one shows the blind.
There is the pact
of dismay,

the nuisance
congratulations,
the Honolulu marriage
of insouciance
with air-age
impatience;

then quiet:
it enters in
dispatches;
recondite
pencil scratches
on onionskin

distance
the comradery.
Someone leaves to shower
dentist's hands'
pinkness and power
into his body,

shedding his *Brattleboro*
Vermont
News,
which no one may borrow,
and whose
account

of early frost
sanctions hope
of knuckles bitten
and fingers crossed
in a mitten.
Envelope

glue on his spit,
a Fauve
works a sketch
around the slit
he cannot stretch
the hymen of.

He draws woodpeckers
smoking cigales,
copies cartoon characters
in lacquers
on Amtrak doors
from decals

on the gimmick
vorpal
plastic rifle butt
trying to mimic
walnut.
Rains topple

the terminal
men's room masonry
and slake
the urinal
camphor cake.
The visionary

builds his stasis
around some token,
afraid
eyeglasses
wormed from Medicaid
will get broken

to uncork
a tunnel,
where he'll find
pork
rind.
Their funnel

was last attack's
dud grenade
caul.
Their backs
tamped a wall
to suede.

It's like a boot
with loose
laces.
A tree's root
races
and thews

earth.
You bayonet
tarps, unwad
each berth-
marinade,
vinaigrette-

claustral
with gas.
Then tanks
break muster, rowel,
trailing hanks
of grass.

Their tunnel
belches
and closes.
Our sentinel
exposes
the villagers.

A turret
aims
a cool
trial squirt.
A duck pool
flames,

slack
laser beam
probes eclipse
fire burning back
on the line of drips.
Crates of candy bars redeem

our stooges.
They harangue
the problem
refugees.
An antebellum
Danang

shill
tongues
his bullhorn.
Engineers shrill
over an aileron
and three bucket prongs

of a bulldozer.
Chinooks yank
our squads
away, over the dowzer
nods
of a tank.

The High Tide

She has a bane.
Fish, see her again.
I can't stop prais-
I think about her ways.

My liberated hand is smeared.
A Greek, bright as a slug. Wearing
the village road or wrapped in
a V-black dress...

Once again room where an, an;
dawn sickens me. Heavy wings dice and knuckle.
Angel! angel and playina! A gagged aorta,
a light prison, a field of azure-tinted wheat.

A loud
sound.

Everything is sweet.
A crook as well aor.
A crook as well air.

How I Compose

Librarians
lie on sofas
in the ladies' room.
And there is something about the lighting

the lights dim as the conductor raises his baton
conduct is still at issue the conduct of writing
and the enormous friendship of husbands.
Someone I admire

wrote a great pile
of French prose
for exercise.
Scrapbooks served me

and staring at
my typed material.
Not doing anything
has served me.

Blue Tree

I stood
like a blue tree
early in the morning.
The stores were locked about me,

the ghosts of women
tugging at my sleeve;
a smile showed in the foliage
which Joe says he won't shave.

And streetlights
were switching off themselves,
the few stars
doing slow dissolves;

ghosts of women
at doors of post offices
were asking me,
slit for letters, this?

Crossing Deering Oaks Park

I draw my snow cap off
so you can see my age
for I have walked enough
in youthful camouflage

Out of range or charter
my vanity still falls
well within my character
for citing intervals

Muted rose aviator jacket
I had a lean hard body
that was soaked with sweat
dozens of times a day

Now that the sewing machine
has white thread in it
the shroud around my station
is stitched even tighter

The Pastures

Here are
the forests
leafless
and bare

the wide
brown
fields wet
with rain

I still
see your land
as the jewel
in the lane

I see
the green
grass frozen
in the ice

become
a Southern
theme
town

once
I was
in a famous
place

built
in
devotion
and revolt

there used to be
a missionary
aspect
to it

the dry
hemisphere
broadcast
into the wet

there was
a lap
of tangled
yarn

accorded to
entry
into the
horizon

a pasture
that a beast
can sense
lies ahead

precision
soaks away
into the one
sheer beauty

an historic
house
built
of bottles

an after
coming head
between the bucket
seats of a car

it makes no
mind no how
America's
cup is there

I can see it
move across
the network
in real time

primitive
weathervanes
have
bullet holes in them

the skies are
leaden on one
side radiant
on the other

some realist
painter's vast
estate stretches
all about

if it were a farm
and he were a friend
it would confer an
axial sense on me

Susie,

I think of Webster, the subtle way
he's being reduced as a person.

Flabby,
thrilled Americans

flowers
with a rag content

preserves
in a balcony situation

quilted toilet
brush holders

adoption
sunglasses

phased
clothes

the bean supper the
potluck supper yes

you are fooling yourself
at a fashion college in Switzerland.

Abelard

I am a leech;
I am a bowel;
I am a screech
owl.

Save
me from sinecure!
I don't shave
below my tonsure.

Heloise,
they cut off my goods.
I can't see the trees
for the woods.

I can't see your thighs
for our shorn hair.
I can't exercise
despair

like a hunting dog.
Leaves
cover the Decalogue.
I'm wearing out my sleeves

on the granite table.
You are the more
capable
administrator.

Monies

I'm
just
not used
to this slum

and
its Harvard
avant-
garde

with these
monies
to come
from

their
mother
ship in our
yard

Towers

You don't
understand
their
behavior

can
hover
between
past and future.

We'll
pool
our
memories.

Towers
ought
not
arise.

You Read

You have abstraction, the major
weakness.

And you have Keats's sure
apprehension,
signifying suspense.

You have

his sense of the hero of Italy.

And you have a scene with C.M. Bowra
reminding you of the Boccaccio story.

Semyon Lipkin and the Russia That Must Be There Somewhere

HORATIO MORPURGO

'What did I not owe to Russia – it has made me all that I am, from there I inwardly set out, all the home of my instinct, all my inward origin is here!' Thus Rainer Maria Rilke, fretting in Munich in 1915, his brief enthusiasm for the 'incredible War God' all in the past as he watches his pre-war 'open world' closing down all around.

To be twenty-something and reading the Russians in the 1990s felt like a way to participate in the world's 're-opening'. As Europe suddenly doubled in size, so did an uneasy awareness of one's ignorance about everything for so long off bounds. A remaindered edition of the Rilke–Tsvaeteva–Pasternak correspondence, or my first *Uncle Vanya* – in a gloriously grubby little theatre outside Saint-Lazare – all felt like ways to get a fix on this perplexing culture and our new relationship with it.

That must be why the country's long slide to authoritarianism since preoccupied me the way it did. Shocked by the assault on Ukraine but far removed from any of the actual destruction, the war struck at me with a long-overdue question. Why did I, as a young man, react to the collapse of Russian-backed dictatorships across Central and Eastern Europe by immersing myself in the literature of, so to speak, the culprit nation? In fairness to my younger self, Czechs, Poles and Romanians figured largely also. The late lamented Milan Kundera did warn against easy assumptions about Russia. And I heard him. It just didn't suit me to listen.

If you recognise this predicament, I recommend two recent publications. In 1998, Alexandr Solzhenitsyn wrote an essay for *Novy Mir* about a collection of poems published seventeen years earlier. Long before X formerly known as Twitter, Kundera once wrote a novel about slowness and what our abandonment of it was doing to us. Literary culture is slow but sometimes in a good way. Solzhenitsyn's essay together with the poems discussed in it are now available in English and not a moment too soon. *A Close Reading of Fifty-Three Poems by Semyon Izrailevich Lipkin* is published by Hendon Books.

The longest poem included, 'The Technical Lieutenant Quartermaster', recounts the Red Army's chaotic retreat across the Don and eastwards in July 1942. Lipkin was seconded to the 110th Kalmyk Cavalry, which was encircled by the Wehrmacht. His squadron became detached and wandered the steppe behind German lines before rejoining Soviet forces in North Ossetia. Through the poet's eyes, we then witness other eyes, one 'dirty winter's morning... that look out from narrow prison windows / Of the box-car of a strange train, under army escort...'

Lipkin was Jewish but the Kalmyks are Buddhists who settled in Russia after migrating from China in the seventeenth century. They had their own units in the Red Army but after the retreat were condemned en masse as Nazi collaborators. On a single day in December 1943, almost the entire population (about one hundred thousand) was deported to Siberia in cattle trucks. Exception was made for Kalmyk women married to Russians.

In 1941, before the German invasion, thousands of German-speaking Jews and other 'socially unreliable elements' from Bukovina had been deported by the Russians. Only a handful ever returned. In 1944 it was the turn of the Crimean Tatars to be deported after they too were identified as collaborators. And as with the Kalmyks, the territory they vacated was later settled by Russians.

Lipkin's inclusion of those box-cars in his poem of course rendered it unpublishable. He turned to translation from several central-Asia Turkic languages, making their literatures available to any Russian who cared to know. He would in due course be hauled before committees for translating from Kalmyk but was not deterred. He also translated from Abkhaz, Dagestani, Kyrgyz, Farsi, Tatar, Tajik and Uzbek.

His own poetry, mainly circulated in private, was also heavily marked by the national cult of state power. 'Nestor and Saria' tells the story of how Beria personally undertook the murder of Soviet Abkhazia's charismatic leader, Nestor Lakoba, who showed insufficient respect, then had his wife and son tortured and murdered also.

Solikamsk was one of many labour camps in the notorious far northern 'Perm Krai'. Lipkin's poem about it is set in August 1962. It describes the indigenous peoples – Voguls (or Mansi) and Ostyaks – made to bow there, alongside others, 'to Russia's hard currency... The gathering's really international: / Udmurts, Volga Germans, a Cossack...' We are introduced to 'Ukrainians from Transcarpathia, / Who learned a long time ago / That we're blood brothers. / Their children were born on the taiga...' Russian officers meanwhile 'live everywhere and protect us, / Because we need to be watched.'

'Working within existing traditions,' Lipkin 'deliberately aligned himself with poets such as Ivan Bunin: craftsmen, not magi; silver, rather than gold.' He has never enjoyed the fame of a Tsvaeteva or Mandelstam. His first poem was published at the age of fifteen, his last shortly before his death in 2003, but his work was not gathered in book form until the 1990s. A devout Jew, his defiance, of the authorities as of literary fashion, was consistent but quiet. He reached a wider audience only after the USSR collapsed. 'You're right of course, / The deeper the sadness / The quieter it is. / That's why the forest / Seems like a big confessional, / A place to whisper... / We in our wars and peace / Multiply the fumes of speech; / Complaints, confusion, curses / Live among the sensitive plants, / We howl and scream and swear / And they keep silent.'

Vladimir Putin's calculation about the attention span of western electorates may yet prove correct. The calculation is, however, heavily reliant on western ignorance of Ukraine and of Russia's behaviour historically in its 'near abroad'. Literary culture may happen slowly but the number of books being translated from Ukrainian (see editorial March/April 2023) must by now be eating away at some of that ignorance. Tim Snyder's excellent online lectures about the country's history have been watched by hundreds of thousands.

Lipkin's achievement demonstrates that even in those golden days when Soviet Russia felt at liberty to starve, deport, re-educate and otherwise 'denazify' its neighbours, there were writers, veterans of Stalingrad no less, who raised their voices steadily, knowledgeably against it. He saw the horror and said so: the fate of the Kulaks before the war, the mass-rape committed by Russians in Germany at its end, the 'Russia dying behind barbed wire' of its aftermath.

This example of engagement suggests to me that the justifications for the present war are largely based on a single, very simple trick of perspective. Ukraine looms so large in our image of Russia's treatment of its neighbours only because it is the biggest of those neighbours facing our way. Its experience of being Russia's 'blood brother' is in many respects unique. But the branding exercise which left Ukraine in such urgent need of 'denazifying', once you look it up in the Soviet rulebook, is entirely routine.

Piously reading the Russians in our twenties, we miss this, absorbing instead a version of the culture from which national monomania has been carefully removed. I might surely have read *The Cossacks* and *Hadji Murat* a different way but chose to enjoy the story-telling. Comparisons may be invidious but modern Russia's record on racism and cattle-trucks is by any reckoning right up there with the big names. What chiefly distinguishes it from the others in that league table is its now mandatory absence of remorse. Three hundred and sixty educational institutions have been destroyed in Ukraine and more than ten times that number damaged, while the child-killers continue to 'issue statements' and 'address summits'.

Testimony from the Literary Memoirs of Semyon Lipkin has been issued alongside the poems. It contains sketches of Lipkin's relationships with Anna Akhmatova and Marina Tsvetaeva, but 'The Fate of Vasily Grossman', a portrait of his friendship with the novelist, takes up the bulk of it. Readers of *PN Review* may find specially striking its account of the role of literary magazines in supporting the structure of truthfulness as a language is subjected to immense distorting pressures.

The memoir of Grossman was written in 1984, at a time when most of those described in it were long dead. It describes a world that also seemed to have gone: 'In those years,' Lipkin writes, 'the literary environment was more important than it is now (I don't know whether such an environment could be said to exist at all today)'. What if more depends on whether he was right about that than we are in the habit of imagining?

Grossman's first novel had appeared back in 1937, based on his experience of working as a mining engineer in Donetsk. A story about his home town of Berdychiv had been well received: he was already on the way to success when he and Lipkin met, not long before the German invasion. They met again at Stalingrad: Lipkin's admiration for his friend's bravery as a reporter, then, and for his treatment of that experience in his later fiction, was unwavering.

Grossman saw the Second World War not as patriotic but fundamentally as a struggle between Fascism and Internationalism. Victory for the latter, he hoped, would clear Russia's collective conscience, 'cleanse us of the blood of the innocent dispossessed, the blood of 1937.' In 1943 the Russian Army newspaper he was working for rejected an article, 'The Ukraine without Jews'. It was a sign of things to come. Grossman contributed to and helped edit *The Black Book*, sponsored by Stalin at first and intended to reveal the scale of Nazi war crimes uncovered by the Red Army as it advanced west. Stalin later withdrew his support and the book was suppressed.

Grossman's post-war fate, and indeed his own, offered Lipkin an exceptionally clear view of the antisemitism endemic to the Soviet system. Novels and stories went unpublished, plays unperformed. Friends were few. 'It was as if everyone suddenly became profoundly short-sighted. Friends approached him, then walked straight past', reflects Shtrum, Grossman's alter ego in *Life and Fate*. Lipkin (himself a character in the novel, Darensky) recalled Grossman reading him the actual letter his mother wrote from the Berdychiv ghetto, on which the novel's 'last letter' is based.

The phenomenon of course went much wider than any writer and his novel, even one as great as this, as Lipkin was very aware. It took in also the persecution of what were euphemistically termed 'doctors': 'Jewish poets who I had translated were arrested, while on trams, buses and trains, people read about doctors who were murderers and pharmacists who sold drops that infected people with syphilis.'

But the bizarre 'arrest' of *Life and Fate* by State Security officers, the bewilderment of that day, is unforgettably recalled here. Their politeness as they ask where the lavatory is while systematically removing every trace of the book from his flat. 'Maybe it'll be published in two or three hundred years', Grossman is told. In the long letter he wrote to Khrushchev afterwards, about the purposes of art – 'literature is not an echo. It talks in its own way about life and the drama of life...' – his isolation, the crushing one-sidedness of this (Khrushchev of course never answered) are plainly audible as he makes the case for freedom and the role of art in its defence.

He left *Everything Flows* unfinished on his death in 1964, after a decline which Lipkin has no doubts was brought on by his brutal exclusion from Russia's cultural life. Technically it was cancer. His writings faded from view and more than a decade passed before Lipkin began to seek out a foreign publisher for the novel. Its success in French translation finally led to its publication in Russia during the 1980s. Only in 1989 was it safe for Lipkin to add a postscript to the memoir. It explains how, before the novel's 'arrest', Grossman had entrusted him with a typescript, which he had concealed in the attic of a Moscow flat.

*

On state power, a passage is quoted from Grossman's *Armenian Sketchbook*. A statue of Stalin, measuring fifty-two metres together with the pedestal, stood above the city of Yerevan in 1961. During construction, as 'parts of its vast bronze body lay on the ground, the workers building it could stand and walk through Stalin's hollow legs unbowed'. The great man was gone now and Armenians had suggested their preferred outcome with admirable restraint: 'Let the metal that went into the monument regain the original nobility of its nature'. The authorities were reminded also that this colossus had been paid for out of public taxation, so the value of its metal should be returned to the public.

To read these two books is to be reminded of a Russia that must surely be there somewhere, hiding out in the immense hollowness. Through his poetry and friendships, through his translations, Lipkin went on working for the 'open world' even as the national obsessives did everything they could – and they could do much – to keep that world tight shut. There may be those in every age who aspire to stand fifty-two metres high and who seek to arrange the world around their delusional self-image. It does not follow that they should be permitted to succeed.

Four Poems

CARL PHILLIPS

Building the Bonfire

The long day goes under. As usual the dark for a moment
feels like the mind turning, more than half reluctantly,
toward the wider theme that some call history, and others
chance… Treat loneliness as
                                        just another landscape, and
you can make a good life there. Of the moon, how far tonight,
or near, depending. Without either of them having
meant to, they never spoke
                                      again: not just acceptance, but
an insistence on the toss-and-go weather of who they were –
together, and separately – inside. Omens, harbingers,
predictions. It only stands to reason that a broken thing,
if it thrives, thrives brokenly. I walked in the park today,
I found this flower, I've named it
Anyone's Face, Still Soft,
Still Waking…

Three Wishes

Hard to believe we
believed dusk was
a matter simply of
the day's several
shadows lying down
all over again
to become the one
shadow – night –
when within each
night of course there

are also shadows. If I
could, I'd hold you
close forever, I keep
thinking, but don't
say. So much, even
now, still comes down
to appearances.
A man who, in
person at least, I've
never met each
night leaves a message –
the same one – for me

to wake to. I own you,
he says, Say it. It appears
he's right. The far-off
horses are not
far off, anymore –
when they run, they
look like what leaving
morals behind for
victory, I imagine,
feels like: to be a storm,
as it clears.

Under the Whip

For some, dream means prophecy.
For many, though, to dream's almost always
a form of remembering some parts
more intimately about the past
than others. How he turned his head,
for example. How *What's left here,*
anymore, he said, *to be afraid*
of losing? Meanwhile the waves,
still; the usual trees; desire,
famously...There's a point at dusk
when the sky finds the exact color of
being forced to choose between what's
impossible and what's just in a different
way impossible; the moment holds; the stars
haven't one by one reappeared yet.

By Woods

I blew the candle out. I watched the glow
of the wick after, till it disappeared. All my life I've
been told not to make more of what's in front of me
than what's in front of me. And I've tried – I've
tried not to. But *isn't* loneliness, for example, a veil
through which, as through grief, our lives remain
still visible, no less detailed, just differently? Why not
say so, or think it at least, even if to oneself, the way
pity being a stranger and stranger word that I use less

often doesn't mean I don't feel it, like a nest abandoned
but unwavering within the private storm that I call
my body – When has a body, though, ever just been
a body? How did baffled, which used to mean being
publicly humiliated, come to mean confused? As a boy,
I had a doll whose head I tore open, hoping to find
all the thoughts in it; all I found was Maybe, and
Let's hope so, and We'll see. Part of me always thinks
I'm drowning. Help me. Please help that part of me.

Welcome to the Culture Wars

John Sutherland, *Triggered Literature: Cancellation, Stealth Censorship and Cultural Warfare* (Biteback) £18.99.

ANDREW HADFIELD

Only if you have had more than just your head buried in the sand for the last decade can you fail to be aware that a war is taking place in Britain: the culture war. Culture has always been contentious, of course, and it wasn't so long ago that the word 'alternative' was bandied about as a marker of either counter-cultural delight or contempt to describe music, comedy, theatre and so on. Now, it would seem the stakes are much higher and one way to reach the hearts and minds of conservative voters is to declare a 'war on woke', a strategy that is currently likely to be more successful in the pursuit of political office than anything so mundane as economic strategy. The battle ground is the campus, as was always likely to happen after higher education expanded after 1999 – when the Labour Party declared that its aim was to have 50 percent of the population with university degrees (current figures suggest that the goal is not far away). One only has to briefly survey the front pages of *The Times*, the *Telegraph*, the *Express* and the *Mail*, to realize how much editors think that their readers crave stories that demonstrate the philistine lunacy of the 'wokerati'. Extensive freedom of information trawls reveal that the English Department at Wrotersley College of Higher Education have replaced Jane Austen with a graphic novel about the downing of the statue of Edward Colston; and, perhaps even worse, the corresponding unit at Slyborough Polytechnic has placed a trigger warning on *King Lear* because it is violent and ageist.

Should we be concerned? Is what is happening a natural changing of the canonical guard? Certainly the *Guardian* coos with enthusiasm when it reports that the lyrics of Taylor Swift are now the subject of a number of university courses, and openly celebrated the Faber publication of Kate Bush's lyrics as serious poetry ('Wow! Wow! Wow! Wow! Wow! Wow! Unbelievable! / Wow! Wow! Wow! Wow! Wow! Wow! Unbelievable!' – from the song 'Wow'). Time does march on, and it has been many years since most students who took English courses read John Dryden, Alfred Lord Tennyson and William Cowper. Alice Walker, Seamus Heaney and Jeanette Winterson are far more canonical, and have been for ages. In the process, have some serious writers been effectively censored because their views do not correspond to modern sensibilities, and their racist, sexist, elitist, homophobic, transphobic and misogynist opinions cancelled? Should some simply be rewritten a bit so that they can be scrubbed clean and made presentable?

The milder form of response is for dons to place a 'trigger warning' on dodgy texts, alerting students to the offensive nature of the material they are about to read. For those who abhor such practices, this involves criticizing *Romeo and Juliet* for being 'heternormative'; for those who see them as a useful tool, gently alerting readers to material that they might otherwise eschew, it simply makes sense to make readers aware that *Titus Andronicus* is a violent play that contains rape scenes, and *Huckleberry Finn* uses racist language.

These interrelated issues, all part of the 'culture wars', are complicated and need to be taken seriously. Making the past into a version of the present flattens out history – and the history of literature and culture – and eliminates nuance, complexity and debate. Extreme, perhaps caricatured, versions of both positions risk just that. If culture is one great, undifferentiated slab of goodness, from Homer to Virginia Woolf, then what exactly does it tell us – and is it actually worth engaging with, because surely we know what it tells us before we read it? If people in the past were all so thick that they need us to correct them, then one presumes the same case can be made.

Even so, censoring works and providing trigger warnings are quite different actions, but they have the same root cause, which is why John Sutherland links the two in his new study. The title of *Triggering Literature* is a pun that gets to the heart of the matter, as read one way it is the literature that triggers its readers; read another, it is us who pull the trigger as we decide what passes muster. The book contains much more detail of cases – which is useful and provides the evidence for debate – than actual analysis. In the preface the author explains that he has a fairly easy-going understanding of his subject: 'Nominally triggering is the subject (of the book) along with a range of other impositions on the creative act and product: namely, cancellation, prepublication bowdlerization, suppression, "red flagging", semi-tolerance'. That is fine, and the issues are linked, but one might want them separated out too, as there is a great distance between censoring *Lady Chatterley's Lover* (my father, a customs officer in the 1960s, confiscated copies of this prohibited paperback) or *The Satanic Verses* (I bought a copy of that novel from the large stock kept under the counter in a Covent Garden bookshop in the late 1980s), and providing a trigger warning to a book that contains some nasty racist passages like *Decline and Fall* (as I forgot to do when teaching it recently, but fortunately no students complained, either because they weren't all that shocked or because they didn't read it).

Triggering Literature consists of three main sections. The first, 'Signs of the Times: A Calendar', provides a brief history of some recent episodes, beginning with the *Daily Telegraph*'s editorial alerting its readers to the University of Greenwich triggering Coleridge's *The Rime of the Ancient Mariner* because it has descriptions of 'animal death' and 'supernatural possession', as well as *Northanger Abbey* because the novel contains accounts of 'toxic relations and friendships'. Excessive perhaps, and possibly a bit precious, but it shows that the university is taking its duty of care to students seriously (and think about how exposed some institutions have been, undoubtedly with some justice, when they have failed to protect vulnerable, exposed young people, with tragic consequences). It's not as if they banned either literary work.

Part two, 'Machineries', might seem a swerve sideways in exploring the ways in which online platforms monitor the material they enable readers to access, but it is crucial to an understanding of how and why reading is enabled and controlled. 'Goodreads' is undoubtedly the best known of these platforms that crowd source recommendations but then feed these back to their users via the internet, establishing a normative cycle of literary tastes, book consumption and judgement open to all. As bookshops outside the large chains have largely disappeared, the once powerful selection and promotion policies of the retail giants now seem relatively benign and ineffective in comparison. Algorithmic logic has an iron grip on readers' choices. Professor Sutherland gives the example of 'Inclusive Minds' (IM), a powerful, well-meaning organization that 'works with the children's book world to support them in authentic representation' (to quote its own definition), of which I had never heard. It seeks to promote diversity and balance in what children read, an ambition that we should applaud, but in doing so it has to decide what to include and what to exclude from its literary canon, much as university courses do. As Sutherland comments, it is surely hard not to approve of its efforts, 'although it is as easy to resent its hectoring, rigid core, self-righteousness about not what children like but what they should like'. The laudable project of Edith Nesbit and other Fabians, who aimed to establish proper literature for children in the early twentieth century, has mutated into something much more authoritarian. One result has been the rewriting of children's classics by Roald Dahl, Enid Blyton and others to exclude derogatory comment. This has triggered the angry response of purists appalled by the sensitivities of the 'snowflake' generation who, presumably, would insist that Agatha Christie's *And Then There Were None* retain its original title.

The final and longest part of the book is a series of case studies, presented in no particular order. They range from the unsurprising news that *Gone with the Wind* is rather racist, recent opprobrium generated in the conservative press when a new edition contained a preface pointing this out, to the terribly sad case of the teenager Molly Russell, who committed suicide after watching the noirish Netflix series *Riverdale*, her death a factor in the so far aspirational British Online Safety Bill, which could yet be 'the biggest triggering to pertain in cultural history'. Sutherland has a neat short essay on Rudyard Kipling, whose life and work triggers the ire of his many detractors. As part of the National Trust's rethinking of its legacy and duties, Kipling's house, Bateman's, 'was branded as stained by colonialism and the slave trade'. As Sutherland points out, Kipling was a supporter of the empire, which he felt had promoted good throughout the world, in particular through helping to abolish the slave trade. Kipling was also targeted at Manchester University when lines from his famous poem 'If' appeared as part of a mural in the student union foyer. Angry students painted over the lines and replaced them with Maya Angelou's 'Still I Rise', the work of a writer of colour replacing that of one who (to quote the student union's liberation and access officer) 'stands for the opposite of liberation, empowerment and human rights'.

Even more celebrated texts have been issued with trigger warnings or cancelled. Newman University decided that David leering after Bathsheba in her bath and consequently sending her loyal husband, Uriah, to his death at the battlefront so that he can have her, was worthy of an alert (presumably the Leonard Cohen song, 'Hallelujah' should also have one, but that may be saved because relatively few of the mass audiences when it is performed on TV know their Bible as well as theology students). Sutherland rather naughtily suggests that the warning, using the rather mysterious 'SV' symbol, perhaps worked rather like the old cinema classification of 'X', giving the episode a 'hot sex rating' and so encouraging seminar attendance and lively discussion. A similar issue arose at Glasgow University when a lecture on 'Jesus and Cinema' planned to show scenes from *The Passion of Christ* (2004), directed by Mel Gibson, a Sedevacantist Catholic, the sect that believes that the papal see has been vacant since John XXIII proclaimed in 1963 that there should be a reconciliation between Christians and Jews. Gibson was detained by the police on a drink-driving charge in Malibu soon after the film's release and belted out some predictable antisemitic sentiments. The film, however, was a great success, the most profitable Christian film in history, but Sutherland thinks the trigger warning is justified because of its conspicuous violence.

A moving epilogue rounds off the book, with the author lamenting but accepting that his passion for the works of William Makepeace Thackeray is unlikely to be shared by many today, the experience of 'his rich clubman prose rising off the page' not really balancing out his virulent racism (worse than that of Dickens who gets more criticism because he is more celebrated). Professor Sutherland wonders how history will judge Thackeray (the Victorian giant will probably join the ranks of the interesting sub-canonical writers who no one really reads, 'the Grimpen Mire that swallows most of published English literature'), and how he had failed to see the vile element in the author's work ('had I Victorianised myself to the extent that I simply did not see it?'). The book concludes in rather low-key mode, acknowledging that sometimes trigger warnings are useful but that, as the examples throughout demonstrate, it is often hard to know exactly where they should be signalled. Surely, it is fair enough to warn readers about the representation of Fagan in *Oliver Twist* – Dickens himself probably would have agreed as he made amends in *Our Mutual Friend* when a Jewish lady wrote to complain to him. And, if you do not get upset about gollies you really need help. But maybe the *Daily Mail* for once has a point in criticizing the Globe Theatre when it warned its audience that its production of *Romeo and Juliet* contained a suicide, as well as gunshot effects and the use of stage blood. Maybe. However, it's not as if you can't see the play and you can always ignore the warning.

We owe a great debt as readers to John Sutherland, who has worked hard over a very long career to make literature interesting and accessible to both academics and the wider public – not just his beloved Victorians, but he has also drawn attention to literary cruxes, puzzles and conundrums, and helped bring marginalized figures such as Monica Jones, Philip Larkin's sometime muse, into the light. His conclusion that trigger warnings are relatively insignificant features of a wider culture war is surely correct. But it is not very helpful, and leaves the wider issues of censorship, literary judgement, authority and the impact of the digital age to intrude into the story as and when they are required to explain more serious matters. The book also seems to have been written in a hurry and the tone veers from jaunty to sombre and elegiac in ways that are sometimes engaging, sometimes jarring. What we have is a series of juicy anecdotes, enjoyable dispatches from a conflict that is surely set to run and run.

Two Poems

FELICITY SHEEHY

Turning Thirty

No alarm wakes me. I sleep in late.
I am late
for the lark's urgent whistle,
the paper's
skittery print. Another day
in the heat.
I pull berries from long stalks,
eat in the field,
walk to the lake in cut-off shorts,
unminded. No man
watches from the street. I feel full
in my body,
as I did as a girl, my hair dripping,
my legs unshaved,
no makeup veiling my face.
All day I swim
in the deep end, moving through
pools of light,
a dragonfly clipping the surface,
a cicada
uncoiling its cry. I buy ice cream
from a woman
at a stand, then another, watching
her grey hair
glisten in the sun. Late-season cherries,
soft ribbons
of cream. Here I am, with my legs
in the grass.
Here I am, licking my spoon, in summer's
full boom.

What My Father Taught Me About the Stars

Not their names.
Not their sizes.
Their coloured alphabet I learned in college,
scuffing my shoe on the back of some chair.
All that stuff about dust.
I already wiped down screens, cut my hair,
sniffed the leaf-litter of books.
I knew the past fell on all of us, all the time,
catching in our hair, like snow. I knew my father
filled his mind with it,
each night, standing in the field,
tipping the sky into his dark stick
like sand
into an hourglass. I knew that space grew
between us,
all those years,
a darkness in which I watched him
watch the stars. Full, as he taught me,
as nothing always is. With matter. With weight.

Four Poems

JANE HOUSTON

Audaxviator

When the world's most solitary species was found
in the hot, utterly black water of Mponeng mine,
the chat was all about sending it to another planet
to see if it survives. As if it's not lonely enough
two miles underground with no other living thing.

Solutions bring their own problems. Ask any child
who kept a bag packed and a runaway note ready.
I couldn't fit my sister in my bag so never got past
Stone Bridge. And the astronaut's rapture comes,
it seems, in looking back – the jewel in the void!

Strike out, with the competency of bacteria,
or run home, for all we can't fit in the bag?
No sunlight or ecosystem, in complete absence.
Technically alive – sounds like death.

Matter

the fridge is moaning
and the cheese in the fridge is flowing back to the cow
the flour on the shelf is trickling to the field
the book on the table opens
its leaves flutter
and it grows one shaking white flower

the fat stones of the house roll away
and the coast road bears east
to a bright hospital
where I am searching for the gone of you
to crawl back inside
and become again the drops of your body

lemme in

Dope

I did not consider this!
When I hid the plant in the green hedge
I did not reckon with a cow angling
her face over the top to eat
its gently nodding buds.
Don't ask me which cow.
They all look stoned, shuffling
nervously – though a wary cow
is hardly paranoid: we feed them,
we steal their babies. One bellows.

She's not in pain. Cows hide suffering.
By the time you spot a sign – the drooping ear,
the lowered eye – you're too late.
Cow pain is like a body frozen in the permafrost,
emaciated and ancient.
It has tattoos of hoofed mammals,
vertebrae with metastatic lesions.
It is buried alone, in a single mound,
holding out for the afterlife.

Body

Much of what I remember appears to me
now as comic strip – not to read, page-by-page
in a magazine, but as something I must wear,
like a mummy, my limbs bandaged, my feet
wadded into bundles, the frames wrapped
in layers on my skin, covered by other scenes.
What I can see is mostly faded, the speech
bubbles empty. A few are impossibly vivid,
this one – I'm cuddling Mum and she's the kid.
I'm trapped on a trampoline. I'm the dog.
Of that day, I see only one corner, but I feel
its exact colours trapped against me, tree,
nail gloss, bluesky glitter autumn winter.

Two Poems

DILYS ROSE

Memory Foam

The mattress had to go. Never mind that
it was still under guarantee and the stains
were barely discernible; never mind that
it hadn't been cheap – or that she had to pay
to get it to the dump.

There was no argument, though some muttered
that chucking it out was a symbolic gesture
she couldn't afford, what with all the other
costs – predictable and unforeseeable –
that the split entailed.

She wasn't sentimental, and hadn't the least
attachment to springs and batting but
each silent, solitary night she'd find dents
in the memory foam, from a shoulder, an elbow,
an outstretched hand.

At the Museum of Broken Relationships, Zagreb

I go alone, move through cool, hushed,
reverent rooms. The only visitor, I tread
gently, wince when my sandals squeak
on the parquet. Hot bright street noise
chinks in: laughter, horns, the clatter-clink
of café-bars, bells upon wedding bells.

Alongside all the tear-stained valentines,
the hoard of eternity rings, everything
but the kitchen sink bears witness
to the jilted: the garden gnome flung
in a fight, a solitary stiletto, the iron
used to press a bridegroom's suit.

To digest so many tales of woe, takes
time, and the day becomes sleeved
in dove-grey shade. A gauze of sad light
drapes the vitrines. If I, too, found myself
bereft, uncoupled, what should I donate
to this archive of abandonment?

Strict Adultery

Andrew Stauffer, *Byron: A Life in Ten Letters* (Cambridge) £25

JEFFREY MEYERS

Lord Byron's letters are marked by intuitive sympathy, vital energy, intellectual audacity and imaginative intensity. Andrew Stauffer, whose method works brilliantly, explains: 'I have selected for closest attention ten of the most interesting and characteristic letters written between his teenage years and his last weeks in Missolonghi. Each chapter begins with Byron's voice on the page, as if we had opened a letter from the poet himself, followed by an account of the experiences and emotions it touches and its place in the poet's life.'

It's a pleasure to read an academic book that is well written and lively, innovative and interesting. Stauffer extracts the rich ore from the letters, is perceptive about the friendship of Byron and Shelley, and provides an exciting narrative of Byron's tragic involvement in the cause of Greek liberation from the Turks. Three spelling errors should be corrected: Durrants Hotel, Sounion and Koblenz. It's worth noting that Byron's line 'Kill'd by five bullets from an old gun-barrel' inspired Kipling's couplet about the English victim of an Afghan rifle: 'Two thousand pounds of education / Drops to a ten-rupee jezail.'

Byron recalled: 'My poor mother was generally in a rage every day, and used to render me frantic when, in her passion' of self-hatred, she mocked the clubfoot that chained his proud spirit to the dull earth. Stauffer describes the protean personae that emerged from that miserable childhood: 'The troubled little boy from Aberdeen, the overweight and bashful Southwell teen, the louche and scandalous libertine of Cambridge and London, the impassioned wanderer in the Mediterranean world, the Italianate lover in Venice and Ravenna', the Romantic poet and the Greek freedom fighter. Byron's self-damaging character was contradictory and complex, solitary and social, malevolent and sublime: 'Rumors of blasphemy, adultery, sodomy, incest and madness surrounded him'. Cambridge University was nothing more to him than 'a villainous Chaos of Dice and Drunkenness, nothing but Hazard and Burgundy, Hunting, Riot and Racing'. He combined voluptuous indolence with satanic evil, and goody-goody Wordsworth firmly declared: 'The man is insane'.

Byron was also convivial and high-spirited, amusing and flippant, chatty and charming. He published *Childe Harold's Pilgrimage* in 1812 and awoke one morning to find himself famous. Though deeply in debt, the aristocrat refused the enormous sum of £1,000 guineas for his next book, but was later forced to accept payment. He thrived on abuse from the critics, which stirred up controversy and kept his books in the public eye. But the spikey author would not allow his timid publisher, John Murray, to censor his challenging work: 'I will have none of your cutting & slashing. I will battle my way against them all – like a Porcupine.'

His poetical persona was a gloomy compact of melancholy, pride, torment and guilt. In a fearsome image, he compared himself to a 'Scorpion girt by fire', with 'Darkness, above, despair beneath, / Around it flame, within it death!' Stauffer's concise descriptions capture the essence of the poems. In Byron's Turkish tales – 'The Giaour' (non-believer), 'The Bride of Abydos' and 'The Corsair' – 'tyranny defeats love, fathers betray sons, the old order collapses but drags the new one down with it'. Don Juan's adventures are 'relayed in the voice of a sly, flirtatious, digressive narrator whose provocative comments (on love, literature, morals, appetites, aging, fame, religion, politics) compel our attention'.

Byron's adventurous life enhanced his poetic reputation. He kept a filthy menagerie of birds, dogs, monkeys, fox, wolf and tame bear that he 'hugged with all the warmth of fraternal affection!' Like the mythic Greek hero Leander, he swam the Turkish Hellespont from Sestos to Abydos; repeated this epic feat by swimming across the even more difficult Tagus River in Lisbon; and also swam four miles from the Lido to the Grand Canal in Venice.

He was ceremoniously honoured by Ali Pasha, the powerful Ottoman ruler of western Greece: 'He told me to consider him as a father whilst I was in Turkey. Indeed he treated me like a child, sending me almonds & sugared sherbet, fruit & sweetmeats 20 times a day. – He begged me to visit him often, and at night when he was more at leisure.' But his kindness disguised his real character, and Byron added that 'he is a remorseless tyrant, guilty of the most horrible cruelties'.

Byron's sexual scandals in England had forced him into exile. Lady Caroline Lamb, a little volcano, pursued him relentlessly and poured lava through his veins. Knowing his taste for handsome youths, she disguised herself as a boy, slipped past his valet and, with a sheepish expression, gained entrance to his chamber. When thwarted, she threatened him with a knife and cut herself. In 1816 she published a tell-tale novel, *Glenarvon*, portraying the Byronic character as an evil seducer who ruins the life of the innocent fictional Caroline. Another aristocratic lady confessed, 'I am entirely at your mercy – I own it – I give myself up to you... now act as you will'.

While married to Annabella Milbanke, Byron had an incestuous affair with his half-sister Augusta Leigh. The daughter of his father's first marriage, she had a husband and three children. Byron treated Annabella cruelly, staying up late at night with Augusta and dismissing his wife by stating, 'Now I have her, you will find that I can do without *you* – in all ways'. Annabella, with their infant daughter Ada, finally left him. But, Stauffer observes, 'publicly declaring his passion for Augusta and living that truth [with her] would mean ruin for them both: social ostracism, exile, loss of friends, of his publisher, his readers, all'. In April 1816 he left England forever.

While Blake and his wife sat naked in their garden, Wordsworth mooned over Marguerite and Keats was blue-balled by the optimistically named Fanny, Byron seduced more women than all the Romantic poets put together. Noble, handsome, dashing, famous, generous and rich, the supreme egoist scattered his maker's image through the land. While travelling in his luxurious coach, he'd arrive at an inn, summon the chambermaid and take her as if by right. In a letter to Augusta he admitted: 'what could I do? – a foolish girl – in spite of all I could say or do – would come after me... I never loved nor pretended to love her – but a man is a man – & if a girl of eighteen comes prancing to you at all hours – there is but one way'. He loved mobile locales that matched his sexual rhythm, and 'tooled' on the road in a post-chaise, hackney coach and court carriage as well as in a gondola, on a table and under it.

Byron's first great Italian lover was Margarita Cogni. Alluding to Raphael's portrait, he called the baker's wife La Fornarina. She said all Italian women took lovers and was willing to sleep with him. Byron described her as 'a very fine animal – of considerable beauty and energy – with many good & several amusing qualities – but wild as a witch – and fierce as a demon'. He praised her youthful figure, black eyes, ribald humour, sexual enthusiasm and operatic devotion. When he planned to leave her, she threatened him with a knife (like Caroline Lamb) and threw herself into a canal.

Though Byron's affairs were completely carnal, his love poetry was divinely lyrical. He devotedly wrote of a Greek lover:

Maid of Athens, ere we part,
Give, oh give me back my heart!
Or, since that has left my breast,
Keep it now, and take the rest!

Exalting the attraction of another lover, he contrasted the earth and heaven, light and dark:

She walks in beauty, like the night
    Of cloudless climes and starry skies;
And all that's best of dark and bright
    Meet in her aspect and her eyes:
Thus mellow'd to that tender light
        Which heaven to gaudy day denies.

Byron's friendship with Percy Shelley in Switzerland and Italy was poetically stimulating and emotionally complex. Though Byron often portrayed himself as a solitary exile, he was really quite social and eagerly responded to the younger poet. Shelley noted that their intense 'conversation consisted in histories of his wounded feelings, & questions as to my affairs, & great professions of friendship & regard for me'. With surprising naiveté, Shelley said that Byron indulged in 'practices which are not only not named but I believe seldom even conceived in England'. In fact, English society was saturated in sodomy, and every guardsman was keen for wealthy clients. Both thrilled and dejected by his companion, Shelley wrote, 'I despair of rivalling Lord Byron, and there is no other with whom it is worth contending'.

Their sexual entanglements were strangely similar. Byron had simultaneously slept with his wife and half-sister. Shelley, with his wife in England, was sleeping with Mary Godwin and her step-sister Claire Claremont, both aged eighteen. The passionate Claire then pursued and seduced Byron, sealing the bond of Byron and Shelley by sleeping with both of them. When Claire became pregnant with Byron's daughter Allegra, he sent her 'to England to assist in peopling that desolate island'. He wanted Allegra to be with him in Italy, but didn't take care of her. She died, aged five, of typhoid fever in 1822. In another tragic parallel, Shelley's children had also died in Italy: Clara of dysentery in 1818, William of cholera in 1819.

Byron's last attachment and greatest love was for the nineteen-year-old countess Teresa Guiccioli. He described her as 'a sort of Italian Caroline Lamb, except that she is much prettier, and not so savage. – But she has the same red-hot head – the same noble disdain of public opinion.' Teresa confessed: 'I felt attracted to him by an irresistible force... I was strong enough to resist at that first encounter, but was so imprudent as to repeat it the next day, when my strength gave way – for B. was not a man to confine himself to sentiment.'

Teresa's wealthy, volatile husband, fifty years older, seemed complacent. But Byron, often threatened with knives, feared he might 'come away with a stiletto in [his] gizzard some fine afternoon'. He practiced 'strict adultery' but became jealous and warned Teresa, who occasionally had to sleep with her husband, 'if you go back to yielding to his false blandishments and dotardly caresses, it is you who will be to blame'. Finally, weary of his servile role, he left for Greece. He expressed his feelings in a famous farewell lyric:

So, we'll go no more a roving
So late into the night,
Though the heart be still as loving,
And the moon be still as bright.

For the sword outwears its sheath,
And the soul wears out the breast,
And the heart must pause to breathe,
And love itself have rest.

Though the night was made for loving,
And the day returns too soon,
Yet we'll go no more a roving
By the light of the moon.

Byron described Teresa's brother Pietro Gamba as 'a very fine spirited young fellow... eager to go to Greece – and very desirous to accompany me'. Byron maintained his emotional connection to Teresa when Pietro joined him in Greece. The friendship of Hemingway, the Byron of our time, with Gianfranco Ivancich, younger brother of his chaste but scandalous Venetian love Adriana, provided the same vicarious sex as Byron's Venetian friendship with Teresa's brother. Both young men were warriors: Pietro fought with the revolutionary patriots in Greece; Gianfranco fought with the Italians in the Second World War.

Byron's money, weapons and leadership encouraged the Greeks to rise against Ottoman oppression. He used his wealth and influence to alleviate the suffering of both Greeks and Turks, and backed Alexandros Mavrocordatos, who later became an important official in the Greek government. Byron saw himself as a Scottish Highland chief who could unite the quarrelling factions against their common enemy, and many people hoped he would become emperor of Greece. But when he paid men their salary and the time for battle dawned, they refused to fight: the fleet sailed home and the soldiers marched away.

He had two narrow escapes en route to Greece. His ship was captured by the Turks but soon released, and he survived a shipwreck when a storm forced him onto the rocks. But he did not survive the third crisis. He wrote that in Missolonghi on 15 February 1824 he had an epileptic fit, 'a strong and sudden convulsive attack which left me speechless though not motionless – for some strong men could not hold me... It was very unpleasant – and nearly carried me off.' After another violent attack of malaria or rheumatic fever, the doctors, despite his vehement objections, were determined to bleed and purge him. He eventually gave in to their demands and shouted, 'Come: you damned set of butchers; take away as much blood as you will; but have done with it.' Free to act, they purged him with castor oil, Epsom salts and enemas, and left him fatally dehydrated and exhausted. He muttered his last words, 'I want to sleep now', and died on 19 April. Byron had the most fascinating character and life of any British poet. With fire, passion and wit he made world history and is still revered in Greece.

Five Poems

BETSY ROSENBERG

Cave of the Bat

Whoever he was I
call him
Heck
or maybe
Kheck
the proto-shaman
laid to rest outside the Cave of the Bat
with a pair of antlers
and the salutary slab of basalt
he toted
all the way
from the hills where he met his
mate, her name was me –
O Kheck....

The Scream

It's late and
while I work I
listen to the intermezzo from
Cavalleria Rusticana –
Yes, I remember,
waiting in the wings
for my cue to run across the stage
and scream
Ahhhhhhhhhhhh
Hanno ammazzato compare
Tur-
iiiiiiiiiid-
du
Who murdered Turiddu
and why?
How should I know,
I'm just an extra,
a Sicilian
woman of the people
in a dress and apron,
didn't even read the libretto
but after this
I can hie me back to the dorm
and tackle the assignment:
Discuss 19th-century Realism,
the literary conventions of
mimesis,
diegesis

And many years down the line I'm
Maria somebody in a
radio play at the climax of which
I'm supposed to scream but
not having read the script
I don't know why
and Morgan the old pro
is just going through the motions
or perhaps he's in distress,
those awful cigarettes
one after another,
the bitter brandy on his breath, and
when he cues me in
I, Maria somebody, turn my head
away from the bi-directional mic
and scream
Ahhhhhhhhhh
and he gives a
thumbs up so
I can hie me home.

Remember the night when
Daddy died
and we stood in a row
the little ones and the big ones
and screamed out of nowhere
Ahhhhhhhhhhhhhhh
Ahhhhhhhhhhhhhhh
Ahhhhhhhhhhhhhhh

Rusalka

Odskocz, odskocz,
the color of peat
flows the Labe over a hunger stone
presaging war and drought
drought and pestilence.
I saw it at dawn
so close to the water line
I cried
and you cried
with me
shapeshifting into Rusalka
ululaio dying moon,
O magic
O melos
my own

Minnie the Moocher

Now here's some discouraging blues for you
with muted trumpet
in a minor key
and the call and response of
Afro-Jewish stars while
dog-eared ghouls and skeletons
slide deftly down the
hi-de-hi-de-
lirium of Chinatown, and
poo-oor Min', doomed to die of influenza,
is dressed like a hoochie-coocher as she
mooches with Smokey the Kokie
on their wedding day to
galaxy Glass-z13
billions and billions of light-years away.

Lullaby for the Newborn Moon

Jupiter, a gleam in the night
between the rain-washed carob trees
at the roundabout,
sixty degrees from the silver crescent
and me on earth in my patent leather shoes,
and a mood imbued with
the 'rueful mien' of a Russian prince,
hair the color of the moon
burnished eyes,
equal in velocity
to the speed of starlight, shifting gravity
from here
to the infinitely far.

Reviews

The Captive Mind

Eva Hoffman, *On Czesław Miłosz: Visions from the Other Europe* (Princeton) £18.99
Reviewed by Tony Roberts

Among the frustrations in Czesław Miłosz's life – and there were as many as there were ironies – were his need to make what he saw as the culturally threadbare America his home and his reputation in the West as an anti-communist writer (*The Captive Mind*) rather than as a poet. Added to that he felt uncomfortable, he told Ewa Czarnecka at the end of their book-length conversation, being known as a noble poet of witness ('I never wanted to be involved in history'). He was, rather, a meditative poet, he said.

Further, Miłosz wrote in Polish but considered himself Lithuanian and bore a bad conscience from the time he served in the Soviet-controlled Polish diplomatic service in Paris and Washington (1946). For that, his reputation in Poland remained poor for many years. Witness his *Guardian* obituary from 2004, where Adam Czerniawski called him 'perhaps the luckiest Polish writer of the last century', one who 'could never understand that by choosing a life of high exposure and ideological manoeuvring, he was bound to provoke hostile reactions, as well as fierce loyalties'.

Then, in 1980, Miłosz was plucked almost from obscurity, at a time when the international focus fixed on Polish affairs (with the *Solidarity* union), when he was awarded the Nobel Prize for Literature. Fame and forgiveness flowed. He returned 'home' in triumph and lived to be feted internationally. His huge *Collected Poems (1931–2001)* was followed a decade later by a sturdy biography by Andrzej Franaszek and, recently, one on his Californian years by Cynthia L. Haven.

It is this controversial character that Eva Hoffman returns to in *On Czesław Miłosz*. Her perspective is that of a fellow exiled Pole whose (slightly later) experience can corroborate and critique his. To this end she weaves herself into his story. Central to her portrait of this man is that 'His poetic principles trumped all other considerations'.

She puzzles over the Miłosz of the war years, seeing 'his determination to retain his distance from events' as excessive, but then surmises that such detachment lay 'not in indifference, but in an intensity of feeling too deep for sorrow – or even tragic lament'. Her other veiled criticism comes with consideration of the 'Soviet' Miłosz. Again, his sense of his destiny as a poet prevailed.

Hoffman is very good on the alienating effects of exile. She suggests, for example, that Miłosz's 'sense of an unattainable reality' was 'magnified' by it, as was his feeling of 'internal emptiness'. To Hoffman, 'great loss, juxtaposed with a moment of evanescent presence' are 'the two polarities driving so much of his poetry'. They are productive of innumerable, unanswerable questions. The 'imperative to remember', in fact, becomes 'an instrument and aspect of morality'.

Although not a poet, Hoffman is intimate with the 'rich oddity' of Polish literature and therefore the context of Miłosz's poetry. Her book brings to life the anguish of exile and, largely, this great, neo-classical poet – one finally rescued by translation – who could never escape his ghosts.

O Thresholds

Leontia Flynn, *Taking Liberties* (Cape), £12
Susannah Dickey, *ISDAL* (Picador), £10.99
Reviewed by Tara Bergin

If the 'company bosses' (as Leontia Flynn calls them in her poem 'All of the people') had more than an inkling of what poetry was capable of, maybe they'd stop using the word 'poetic' to describe their luxury tissues or shades of emulsion paint. If they suspected that 'poetry' constituted searing interrogations of their own slapdash behaviour – as exemplified in these two new collections – then they might run a mile from the descriptor. These poets chew their bread, as Paul Celan put it, 'with writing teeth': grinding, assessing. Their work is nothing like the floaty vagueness of elegant advertising. It's built from what W.G. Sebald once described as 'acute, merciless observation' and is stark, crafted, funny and real.

I first heard abut Leontia Flynn's fifth collection, *Taking Liberties*, on the grapevine. Someone actually said to me outside a pub, 'have you heard Leontia Flynn's new poem about her cat? It's amazing.' Such gossip speaks not just of Flynn's importance as a writer, but also of her success in maintaining a sense of newness and freshness. The poems display a combination of caring deeply and not at all; they are tender and barbed, irritable and longing, all at the same time.

The book itself is pleasantly laid out: a black-and-white photograph by Anton Atanasov on the cover, showing train tracks disappearing into the mist to illustrate the title's suggestion of freedom, and of 'stealing' away. Inside are the epigraphs, the list of contents, and about sixty pages of poems. Sounds normal enough, but the first rebellion, or 'liberty taken', appears in the epigraphs: one by George Sand, advocating travel; one by Chaucer, advocating freedom from marriage; and one by Vladimir Putin, stating: 'The liberal idea has become obsolete. It has come into conflict with the interests of the overwhelming majority of the population.' It's a horrible yet necessary quote, and the three epigraphs taken together act as both a warning and a promise of what's to come. These poems examine and reflect the world: the people who control it; those who live and try to survive in it; the way people navigate it.

The collection opens with 'Mid-term in Belfast', it's spring, magnolia trees are in bud, the menorah 'lifts its arms / under plane trail / and cloud scud'. But the plan is uncertain, children are crying, some items are gathered 'and thrown, in haste, in the trunk'. From here, we the reader (whom Flynn looks in the eye in a thrilling sequence called 'On platforms and in plate-glass waiting rooms', and addresses as 'the border') – find ourselves in an Irish motorway service station, a Parisian public square, a Canadian arts centre, a Newfoundland guesthouse, a hospital, a bedroom, the bank of a river. We are upstairs looking out, we are outside looking in, and of course, we are fallen, down on the ground, having tripped on the road to perdition where 'no step seems irrevocable... "Is this tragic, is this tragic?" you think, "No this is not tragic" – picking yourself up from the crystal shards, and readjusting your sleeves.'

When I laugh at these poems it's not because they 'amuse' me as such, but because they are right, witty, insightful and sharp. When I am moved by them, it's not because they are sentimental or 'warming' – on the contrary. I'm moved because the poems are written with a clear eye, a clear ear, and an equal measure of grace and grit. Take, for example, 'In classrooms and in science labs'. The title doesn't give anything away: none of the titles in the collection do; they are merely the first line of the poem. But the story that the poem tells is of the Uvalde school shooting in Texas. At the end of the poem, the image of a mother running to the school gate merges with the image of a crucifixion:

> I ran, I ran barefoot
> my husband beside me
>
> with my flimsy sandals
> held in my hands
> till I came to the gates
>
> [...]
>
> A mile through the streets
> clutching my sandals
> I ran to the gates
> the foot of the cross
>
> *You must build a wall*
> *round the soul of your child*
> but in my heart
> the assailant had entered.

The use of repetition, the focus on the flimsy sandals, the bare feet, the running towards 'the gates' which become 'the foot of the cross', make this hit as powerfully as the most effective kind of reportage.

And then there is the infamous 'Cat Poem' ('The cat is pure of heart') as well as the 'Tortoise Poem', the 'Budgie Poem' and even the 'Houseplant Poem' ('the houseplants are private'). These fourteen-liners come at the end of the book, and act as moments (monuments) of reprieve and recovery: a brief respite from 'the gradual breakdown'... the 'hot crucible of love / and self-annihilation' that is so unflinchingly presented throughout this brilliant fifth collection.

*

Which brings me neatly to *ISDAL*, the debut collection by Susannah Dickey, a writer who manages to create poems by both embracing and shattering some of poetry's key characteristics. Inside its punkish pink and black covers we find brevity, fragment, repetition, simile, imagery, rhythm and voice. We find refrain. But we also find a nameless murdered woman, two cheeky podcast presenters, filmic scenarios, weird dreams, Norwegian landscapes, intimate exchanges and probing questions about the media's obsession with naked dead females.

For example, here is a quote from one disarming poem, 'Dream of a postmortem'. Warning, it's not 'easy' reading:

> Her insides opening with the thick vapour of maraschino
> acid. Her intestines are marinade sinister. Perhaps her uterus
> looked like an attacked vine tomato. Lilting and neglected.
> Hocked salsa and old potatoes.
> How sordid is it to invent a reason to put hands in a woman?

The description is hard to stomach but its formality and directness are admirable. The poem ends with an observation, ironic but also scary: 'How unnecessary, perhaps, to kill a woman. So soft / but so un-mummed. So fabulous.' It's not clear whether the 'fabulous' refers to the woman or the killing.

The layout of this book plays with convention. Its three parts are named 'Podcast', 'Narrative' and 'Composite', and within each section we find an array of forms and formats: poems placed at the bottom half of the page rather than the top, poems whose titles are just ellipses in square brackets, poems with dashes and gaps and asterisks, poems that look like transcripts of a dialogue, a set of essay-style poems. It's interesting and energising. Here is the poem, '* Outtake #8' quoted in its entirety:

> Can it be voyeurism if she's already dead?
> I don't know.
> But.
> What?
> In recruiting this harem of voyeurs we've diverted them from –
> From what?

If this reads slightly flat, that's good. These 'Outtakes' depict a casualness that is shocking because it's ordinary and familiar. You'll have guessed by now that like *Taking Liberties*, *ISDAL* is not the collection you'll go to for 'happy fluffiness' (as one mother in the swimming-pool café described her literary requirements to me), but if you care about human psychology you will find a strange comfort here – in the nature of the inquiry, the spirit of the adventure, and the conscientiousness of the language used to explore it.

This is a very 'contemporary' poetry book, with its cool presentation, its fiercely intelligent voice and eye, and its timely subject-matter. It captures the moment. When I told a friend I was reading a new poetry collection that was 'a kind of Scandi-Noir with podcast outtakes that questions media's fascination with dead naked women', her reaction was: 'I love it already'. But it's also a book that displays linguistic deftness, dexterity and confidence. It's crime-poetry; it's forensic-lyricism; it's sensual, creepy, insistent, revealing. It takes stock of us.

The collection ends with a sequence of poems that the poet categorises as 'Composites'. These are thoughtful explorations into ideas of perception; they make statements, they are curious about how we see the world: 'The sun and moon were the same size to you once... Size is fallible as time'. These final poems go to the heart of the matter. On the last page is this observation: 'There is no homogeneity of response to pain but what if there were / and it was this: standing under September's last // ripe sky'. It just so happens that I was reading this poem right at the end of September, and I noticed that the description fitted perfectly.

The Picture Refigured

Lucy Hamilton, *Viewer* | *Viewed* (Shearsman) £10.95
Reviewed by Ian Seed

Lucy Hamilton's *Viewer* | *Viewed* comprises a series of poems written in long-lined couplets alongside a series of photomontages of herself, members of her family, friends, and objects such as flowers, letters, heirlooms, medieval images and snippets of literature. It is an endeavour which could so easily have fallen into cliché, sentimentality or over-abstraction in the hands of a lesser poet. As Hamilton herself admits, reflecting on the risks,

the poem depends| the verse suspended| all contingent
on the picture| A double act to find or fall| To hang

on the wall or abort| ('Picture Not Found | Poem Not Housed')

In her Preface, Hamilton explains that when a close friend unexpectedly died in 2014, she found herself 'unable to write' and thus 'began making photomontages by hand as an alternative method of expression'. Her concern, she says, is 'not / meaning not even aesthetic value' but to 'invite the tug // of juxtaposition' ('An Old Story'). This may have been a starting point for Hamilton, but it is clear that aesthetic value is in fact of prime importance in the crafting of these photomontages and poems.

The writer's block that Hamilton describes may have also been due to something that most of us have difficulty with, namely stepping outside the set stories of our lives we so often tell ourselves. The use of collage, reinforced by the sheer physicality of cutting up materials and pasting them back together in new and strange ways, provides us with the means to reimagine our concept of ourselves and our relations with others. We are given the lens to view events, including our deepest losses, in a wider spatial and temporal context.

The photomontages themselves, in part influenced by the work of the conceptual artist John Stezaker, for example the splicing of two faces together, are astonishingly beguiling. Entering the world of *Viewer | Viewed* is like stepping into a gallery where you want to linger on each artefact for as long as you can because each one offers so many different perspectives on the same set of objects. The accompanying couplets are perfectly paced, leaving space for us to complete the fuller stories for ourselves. Hamilton masterfully moves from reflection on the process of photomontage and its resulting images to description and reflection on her own life. The use of vertical lines instead of commas and full stops reinforces the sense of the fragmented nature of our thought processes and memories. One can envision the lines as scissor blades cutting up a clichéd story and rearranging it into something unexpectedly profound and spellbinding.

The opening poem, 'Refiguring the Picture', sets the tone for the work that follows. It begins with the poet asking herself how to split the heads of herself and her twin sister, aged six, in a seaside photo ('a question of wet pigtails / tied behind the ears') and then to go about 'jiggling two-half-faces together for optimum fit / touching up the ribbons with brush and ink'. The poem subsequently travels back to the time when the twins were separate eggs in their mother's womb, and speculates on the possible scientific reasons why one twin had problems with being breastfed, thus 'creating a fret of presence & absence' in the other. After that, the poem returns to the collage process of tinting the photos of the ribbons 'in the colours they were given' before ending with a couplet, which, with its beautifully concrete imagery, reveals the close bond between the two sisters, without ever letting us forget that this is the poet reimagining as well as remembering: 'Among the off-cuts| two salty hands that shared the womb / continue to grasp each other| elated after the swim'.

As well as portraits of her twin sister, there are several of other members of Hamilton's family and friends, for example her brother whose face is juxtaposed with a 'leaf's veined epidermis' which 'foreshadows the organ he will lose to a tumour' ('Gold Leaf Boy'); her father who as a boy in a cut-out photo holds a 'cow by a staff attached / to its nose ring' ('Farm Boy on the Wirral'); and her French mother who is no longer alive to 'see my homage pastiche of herself/arch/map', but who 'knew Picasso & / Braque in her native Paris' ('*MASHUP* | MONTAGE'*)*.

Lucy Hamilton's *Viewer | Viewed* is a distinctive and powerful collection, challenging us to re-vision our own lives, and to celebrate the sheer fact of having lived.

Terms and Conditions

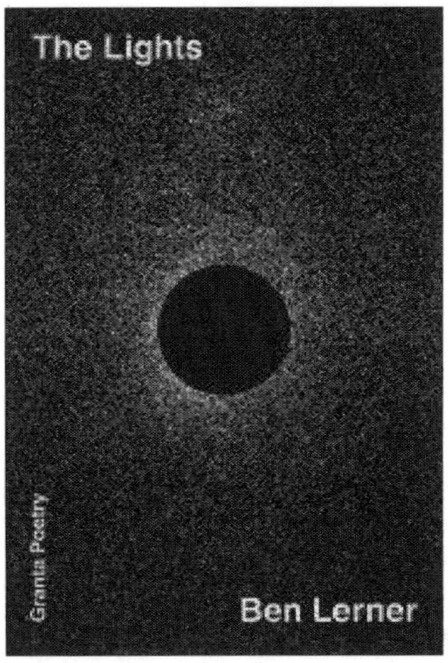

Ben Lerner, *The Lights* (Granta) $12.99
Reviewed by Dane Holt

The internal architecture of *The Lights*, Ben Lerner's most recent collection, deserves its own review. In order to fool a reader into thinking that a collection of poems is more meticulously structured than it actually is, the poet might take a few tried-and-tested shortcuts: certain images reoccur, a phrase gets modulated here and there. *The Lights*, however, encourages reading from front to back then resists it, until you're travelling back and forth, finding new avenues, forging alternate paths in which crops of imagery, entire rhythms, stanza shapes, tones of voice and ideas are altered, often significantly, out of their original proportions.

Lerner is helpful in the initial stages of the trip by providing an 'Index of Themes' as the opening poem: 'Poems about night / and related poems. [...] Poems about you, prose / poems.' The book moves between these two modes, playing one off the other like light off shadow or, as in 'Contre-Jour', 'light that changes / the light that goes out'. The discursive range of the prose (like Lerner I struggle to fully commit to calling them prose poems) is remarkable in its capacity, its frame of reference, its self-contradiction – 'She looked at me to ascertain if I was being serious or merely difficult' ('The Grove') – while never betraying narrative momentum. One prose piece, 'The Chorus', is perhaps the most straightforward in terms of its movement from A to B. It recounts an episode in which Benner (the father's name for the young Ben) is unable, as the only Jewish child in the class, to separate himself from his peers during a Christmas recital. The situation is made worse by the father's patience and understanding: 'What I've learned is that the hardest part of the winter concert for you is the worry itself – that once you get up there on the stage you do a great job and you have a good feeling afterward. But like I said it's up to you. When I was a kid, my dad was way too intense about this kind of thing'. This passage encapsulates much of Lerner's concerns about the act of poetry itself: how can the singer's voice be removed from the song and the song still survive? 'You cannot withdraw and sing, at least not intelligibly' ('Autotune'). Elsewhere, the concern becomes material: 'I was going to praise the transpersonality of print over the individuality of handwriting' ('Rotation').

The prose pieces ignite the concentration of the lyrics and their intention, as 'Meridian Response' puts it, to articulate 'the nearly audible': 'click of snow / on snow', 'a recording / of rain stopping, power being cut', 'the almost / sound when deer look up'. Such momentary acoustical almost-phenomena are adjacent to John Stewart Mill's definition of the lyric as 'overheard speech'. Of course, Mill defined it as much more besides and so does Lerner. Attempts at definition are the book's primary preoccupation: definitions of poetry, of song, of singing, of speech, of talking; defining limits of communication, of public speech and private, of self and non-human selfhood: 'I want to sing of the seismic activity deep in the earth and the destruction of the earth for profit / in a voice whose particularity has been extracted by machine'. Even definitions of writer and reader are troubled: 'the goal is to be on both sides of the poem, / shuttling between the you and I' ('The Dark Threw Patches Down Upon Me Also'). Lerner proposes these new modes of interaction. It is true of all great poems and books of poems that they ask us to accept a new set of the terms and conditions.

On Nothing in Particular

The Penguin Book of Elegy: Poems of Memory, Mourning, and Consolation, edited by Andrew Motion and Stephen Regan (Penguin Classics) £40
Reviewed by Jack Barron

William Empson's poem 'Ignorance of Death' thinks a lot about how to think – or not think – about the end of thought. It takes us through various cultural approaches to death, from Buddhist to Christian to Communist. But in the end – that is, the end of the poem and the end of it all – we find no conclusion, only an appeal to unknowingness, couched typically in that tone of Empsonian table-talk:

> Otherwise I feel very blank upon this topic,
> And think that though important, and proper for anyone to bring up,
> It is one that most people should be prepared to be blank upon.

There is a small and sharp difference between 'I feel very blank' and 'to be blank': the former allows the first person at least some affective response, no matter how unfeeling, with 'very' suggesting the possibility of degree; the latter couples our most fundamental infinitive ('to be') to the ultimate and un-adjectivised blankness that may constitute non-being. The lines thereby describe, with perfect contradictory force, an indefinite end – the final paradox we all must one day meet.

Although Empson's blankness proves a particularly unyielding term with which to deal, it remains a fact that such a contradiction forms the heart of elegiac thinking: that is, the point at which words may fail is precisely where elegy starts its work. It is perhaps unsurprising that taking death – or the process of dying – as a beginning produces an infinitely rich variety of responses, and now *The Penguin Book of Elegy: Poems of Memory, Mourning, and Consolation* has supplied an extensive curation of elegists throughout the ages. The book is edited by earnest and erstwhile Poet Laureate Andrew Motion and Stephen Regan, Professor of English at Durham University, who has a scholarly interest in the elegiac tradition. Between them we have ourselves a poet-critic, which provides the right combination of linguistic alertness and historical imagination necessary for elegy's safe handling.

Indeed, together they have penned a thorough and informative introduction, one that makes great claims on the nature of poetry writ large: 'All poetry exists as a record of life snatched away from the destructive flow of time'; that whisks the reader bracingly through the formal and technical history of elegy, from its metrical origins in Ancient Greek through its bucolic Christian translation; and that provides thoughtful reflections on the figurations of elegiac verse practice: 'elegiac poetry [is often] characterized by a high degree of self-consciousness'. All in all, it is good preparation for the various losses, heartbreaks, ironies and blanks that follow.

The selection of poems itself covers an incredible range. Curiously, our elegists are not arranged chronologically, but rather in alphabetical order. At first this is a little jarring, but – Motion and Regan explain – the decision was designed to encourage the unexpected joys of chance. We therefore find Horace rubbing shoulders with Housman, the Brontë sisters speaking together once again, Swinburne introducing *In Memoriam*, and Stevie Smith responding to John Skelton with chanced felicity.

Thanks to this comprehensive list, the book is an unwieldy object (I keep finding myself referring to it as *Penguin's* Big *Book of Elegy*), and not really something to take on the tube. But this is apt: death is an awkward subject. And the size and span is relevant because our approaches and responses to loss have often been structured with a certain discomfit. Take, for instance, Denise Riley's *A Part Song*, written after and for the loss of her son: 'A wardrobe gapes, a mourner tries / Her several styles of howling-guise'. The couplet – which thinks not only about how we address the dead but how we dress for the dead – is decidedly a little off, a bit awkward: the rhyme comes too easily and therefore rings untrue. But then, what could be more wrong than a mother outliving her son? There is also, haunting this awkwardness, the fact that 'elegy' comes from *elegos*, a metrical form originally consisting of couplets. In choosing couplets here, Riley at once acknowledges tradition and exposes its faults, as it gets jaded – like we all do – by the passing of time. It is a masterly poem and one that proves the necessity of elegy while performing its ceaselessly shifting aspect.

Despite its formidable coverage, there will always be more elegies than can be held in a place such as this. And there are some omissions that deserve mention: D.S. Marriott's 'Goodbye Porkpie Hat', for instance, an elegy for the late great poet Sean Bonney, who died in 2019, which is at once a valediction and protest song; or Keston Sutherland's *The Odes to TL61P*, an elegy for a now-defunct Hotpoint washer-dryer; or J.H. Prynne's elegy for Paul Celan, 'Es Lebe der König', the lines of which build and melt away with the gentlest of similes: 'we too are numbered like / prints in the new snow'. Yet I don't really intend this as a criticism of Motion and Regan. First, because the practical hurdles involved in putting an anthology together must always be acknowledged. It is very possible these poets simply refused to be included (for which Prynne is notorious). And second, and most important, because this feels like evidence of elegy's insistent chimerical existence: of the fact that the singularity of death will always give rise to a greater variety of responses than any one book can contain.

In the end, a book of so many endings will always be a strange object: it is structured by gaps, aporia and doubt, studded with sudden losses. Collected together like this, the milieu of poems comes to describe, as intimately as anything can, the contours of absence: that indefinite shape at the centre of it all. The weight of the book becomes an ironic token of this commonplace absurdity, and a heavy reminder that our reply to the unthinkable is naturally obsessive. Within its pages we find ourselves – mournfully and joyously and blankly and otherwise variously – reading against loss: it is excellent preparation for nothing.

Speaking Sideways

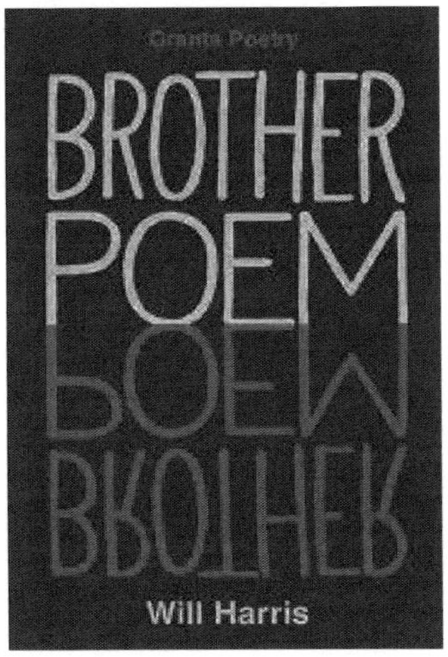

Will Harris, *Brother Poem* (Granta)
Reviewed by Joe Carrick-Varty

I'm always suspicious of poetry that claims to know exactly what on earth is going on. *Brother Poem*, Will Harris's second book, works *because* it relinquishes its knowing. The book achieves a single, extended conceit, one of an imaginary brother who is rendered and rendered again by the poems' speakers, where the act of calling and calling into an absence becomes a form of knowing (or a way of knowing?). And the result? A poetics that cultivates emptiness if only to reach beyond the very end of distance: 'If I can't reach you, let me fold these words into a better / concept of direction'.

It's a fun experiment, one the poet calls 'an experiment in speaking sideways': how far can you push the conceit? How long will you wait for an answer? And, most important of all: what will the echoes sound like? Because the brother-shaped echoes are what lift this book beyond: 'I heard it. And I heard it in your speaking.'

Take the poem 'Weather and Address', where two realities, two timelines echo simultaneously: 'Walking down West Green Road... toggling with street view / and the view itself'. This subtle determination between views allows for distance to collapse and tangible absence to take on the act of filling, instead of merely being filled. So, the poem is calling and answering at once: cool! Again, the speaker, while addressing the brother, uses 'a mode of address / emerging like the weather, not directed at but around us... not looking at you but / at the screen where our eyes met' until the poem ends with the closest thing the book has to an answer: 'because the sky surrounds us falling upwards'.

In this way, *Brother Poem* is a departure from Harris's Forward Prize-winning debut *RENDANG*, in which there was more comfort in narrative determination. But here remains that meandering, thinking-in-action style of voice typical of *RENDANG*, as in 'South London Mum', a hilarious and fantastical poem about gentrification where the act of telling the story becomes the story itself: 'Halfway through our lease, a wealthy couple moved in next / door.'

Perhaps the biggest departure from *RENDANG* is *Brother Poem*'s deployment of wide-ranging sequence. The book contains four sequences, the highlight being the title sequence, a thirty-six-page, unpunctuated address to the speaker's imaginary brother. I love an unruly sequence; I love the way a book can hang, like birds or fairy lights, around such a sequence. I also love to think of books as people, with limbs and organs and a certain inclination towards lifestyle. If *Brother Poem* were a person, they would live in a rainy city, they would step off the bus with their hands buried deep inside their pockets, jacket hitched up against the wind, and, as they called through the grey air to their brother, this is how it would sound:

And as
I walked on
though my life was
broken yes my voice was
heard and it my voice I heard
in a little corner of the room saying
I'll walk with you and leave you with me

Some Contributors

Richard Gwyn is the author of *The Vagabond's Breakfast* (Wales Book of the Year, 2012) and its sequel, *Ambassador of Nowhere: A Latin American Pilgrimage* (2024). As a translator from Spanish, his anthology *The Other Tiger* (2016) has introduced a new generation of Latin American poets to English readers. **Jane Houston** lives in south Wales and has published poems in UK magazines including *Ambit*, *Poetry Wales* and *The Rialto*. **Darío Jaramillo** is one of Colombia's foremost poets and novelists, winner of his country's National Poetry Prize (2017) and of the International Federico García Lorca Prize (2018). His selected poems, *Impossible Loves* (Carcanet, 2019), translated by Richard Gwyn, was shortlisted for the Premio Valle-Inclán in 2020. **Jeffrey Meyers**'s *James Salter: Pilot, Screenwriter, Novelist* and *Parallel Lives: From Freud and Mann to Arbus and Plath* are both forthcoming in 2024 from Louisiana State University Press. **Dilys Rose** is a novelist, short story writer and poet. She has published eight books of fiction and four of poetry, most recently the short story collection *Sea Fret* (Scotland Street Press, 2022) and a poetry pamphlet, *Stone the Crows* (Mariscat Press, 2020). A new poetry collection, *Memory Foam*, is due out in 2024. Currently, she divides her time between writing and printmaking. **Betsy Rosenberg** is a Jerusalem-based translator and editor. Her book of selected poems *A Future More Vivid* was published by Sheep Meadow Press in 2014. **Felicity Sheehy** is a poet from the Hudson Valley of New York. Her chapbook *Losing the Farm* won the Munster Literature Centre's international chapbook prize. Her work has appeared in *The New Republic*, *the Southern Review*, *the Irish Times*, and elsewhere.

Editors
Michael Schmidt
John McAuliffe

Editorial Manager
Andrew Latimer

Contributing Editors
Anthony Vahni Capildeo
Sasha Dugdale
Will Harris

Copyeditor
Maren Meinhardt

Designed by
Andrew Latimer

Editorial address
The Editors at the address on the right. Manuscripts cannot be returned unless accompanied by a stamped addressed envelope or international reply coupon.

Trade distributors
Combined Book Services Ltd

Represented by
Compass IPS Ltd

ISBN 978-1-80017-418-4
ISBN 0144-7076

Subscriptions—6 issues
INDIVIDUAL–print and digital: £45; abroad £65
INSTITUTIONS–print only: £76; abroad £90
INSTITUTIONS–digital only: from Exact Editions (https://shop.exacteditions.com/gb/pn-review)
to: PN Review, Alliance House, 30 Cross Street, Manchester, M2 7AQ, UK.

Supported by
Supported using public funding by ARTS COUNCIL ENGLAND